CRYPTO REVOLUTION

BITCOIN, CRYPTOCURRENCY AND THE FUTURE OF MONEY

How you could make a life-changing fortune buying and holding cryptocurrencies

SAM VOLKERING

Printed March 2020

ISBN 978 1 9162 0913 8

Edited by: Kelly Buckley
Design and layout by: Dean Murphy

Crypto Revolution: Bitcoin, Cryptocurrency and the Future of Money

Foreword

Man is born free, and everywhere he is in chains. One man thinks himself the master of others, but remains more of a slave than they are.

– Jean-Jacques Rousseau

I bet you've probably heard the first part of this quote but not the second. It's so often the case that the sound bite which gets repeated is often a trite quip while the rest, of what in this case Rousseau had to say, is infinitely more important.

The reality is that we live in a society where a small group of people think they know better than we do how we should live our lives. They don't ever seem to realise that the power and wealth they surround themselves with is only possible because of the quiet acquiescence of the majority.

Very occasionally there is a turning point where the silent endurers rise up and shake off the shackles they have been forced to bear by sanctimonious know-it-alls and reassert their right to freedom of thought, expression and control of the fruits of their labour.

Cryptocurrencies and Sam Volkering came along at just the right time. We have been through a torrid decade and more, where living standards have declined but we are constantly told this is one of the longest running economic expansions in history. It's as if we truly live in George Orwell's *1984* and the powers that be speak a form of doublespeak.

When they say employment is at a record high they fail to say wages have been going down in real terms for decades. When they say it's the longest expansion since they started measuring, they fail to say it was because the economy was coming off its knees and every point of growth was bought by robbing savers of their income. When they say we are producing more energy from renewable sources than ever, they fail to say North Sea oil is in decline and we are importing more energy than ever.

You get the picture. We are constantly being told how great everything is but we know in our bones it's not true. But it could be... and through technology it will be.

There is only one answer to political and financial problems that assail us. Step outside the circus.

That's where cryptocurrencies come in. The good news is they cannot be lent into existence. There is limited supply and the uses to which they are being put are growing at an exponential rate. Did I mention they offer a secure form of transferring or recording ownership of your assets and they function completely independently of governments?

That's why this is an important book. Sam has done a great job of laying out why you need to know more about this rapidly evolving sector. I first met Sam shortly after joining the Southbank Investment Research team and I was impressed by his resolve to do his very best for our clients as we attempt to guide you to a more profitable future.

However, the truth is that cryptocurrencies represent one of the biggest bull markets in history and this boom is the only thing that comes close to the California Gold Rush. Back in the 1840s the '49ers traipsed across the US to get their piece of the golden bounty that lay beneath California's hills. Today a similar trend is driving the desire of many people to both own and 'mine' cryptocurrencies.

Rather than leave the comfort of your home, with a powerful computer and ample electricity you can create your own mine and get your piece of this bull market. It's totally egalitarian. You don't need a degree or qualifications and it doesn't matter who you know or what school you went to. Cryptocurrencies are open to everyone, and that is why the monetary authorities are so wary of them.

Cryptocurrencies wrest control from the grasp of the financial elite because they cannot control supply. That's the equivalent of setting up a new standard for value, which we might argue is appropriate for a modern age. The gold standard functioned for millennia, or for as long as we were dependent on extractive resources to generate wealth. Isn't it worth considering that it is time for a digital asset in a world where value is increasingly tied to data and how it is manipulated?

Even if you never end up buying a Bitcoin, Ethereum or Ripple, you have to know that other people will. Understanding what motivates individuals to seek radical freedom is important because as the market grows, it will make its way into the public sphere and if you are not up to date you will be left behind. That's reason enough to read and enjoy this book.

Eoin Treacy
Investment Director, *Frontier Tech Investor*

PART ONE: Life story

Chapter 1: Your first thing to do: make a choice

Mania. Hysteria. Chaos. Confusion. Turmoil. The end of the world as we know it. GFC 2.0. The world you live in today has never been as tense, as volatile, as scary or as pessimistic in any time prior.

Every night on the news you hear of terror attacks, bombings, death, destruction and the erosion of your free world. Countries are turning away from each other and into themselves. Globalisation is giving way to isolationism and nationalism.

We're more politically correct than ever before. We must not offend. We must not step outside the 'norm'. We must abide by what our elected officials deem are the rules of the game... except those rules are tilted to their favour and not the average person who just wants to make their way in the world.

Meanwhile the "establishment" continues to grow in power and wealth. They pay less tax than you. They break the rules more than you – but get away with nothing more than a slap on the wrists, if they even get caught. They gather the wealth of the world more than you.

They built the game and the game rewards them handsomely. But what has the game ever done for you? While the rich get richer, the power brokers get more power, where does that leave someone like you?

Think about it. When have you ever seen tangible benefit from the financial system that's built around you? Do you still toil away nine-to-five to put food on the table, pay the mortgage and enjoy a semblance of a fun and happy life?

Do you bust your back to try and get ahead in the world, all the while seemingly having a huge chunk of your wealth taken away by the government, the actions of erroneous fund managers, bankers and the welfare state? Money that you'll never see a dime of?

You only need to answer yes to just one of those questions to be in a position that, at the end of this book, might be radically different.

Right now you are sitting through the most significant revolution in finance, economics, investment, wealth and social architecture in the history of the world.

You're alive at a moment in time that we'll likely never see again. A once-in-a-lifetime situation, when everything the establishment have built to benefit themselves comes crashing down around them.

But this isn't some almighty global financial crisis (although that might be a factor). This isn't a situation where you should worry, be scared or feel under threat. In fact, quite the opposite.

This is an opportunity where the average person, someone like you, has a chance to get involved in a revolution of wealth and finance that destroys the traditional conventions of wealth, investment, savings and even the very definition of money, currency and power.

You're alive at the beginning of the "crypto revolution". The birth and growth of the crypto economy, cryptocurrencies, crypto assets, digital assets – the biggest technological advancement since the internet.

You're alive in a time of incredible opportunity, optimism and an environment for growth that you'll probably never see again or have another chance to capitalise from.

Today is the time when you can take a chance, roll the dice. Be smart, shrewd and focused on the enormity of opportunity in front of you. Today is the day you immerse yourself in all things "crypto" and open your life, wealth and future to the possibilities that the establishment doesn't see, doesn't understand. And when they wake up to it, they will be petrified of it.

Today is your chance to "stick it to the man". To stick it to the establishment. Today is the day you make a choice. It's a simple choice. And it's a choice you'll never get again.

Choice 1: Read the rest of this book, word by word, line by line, chapter by chapter. Maybe even read it a few times to understand it all. And by the end of it be prepared, armed, educated on the crypto opportunity.

Choice 2: Read this book in part. Probably skim through, and don't read it all. Dismiss the ideas, facts, concepts as a fad, a bubble, "fake internet money" or simply worthless. Put the idea of anything to do with crypto aside. But in doing so possibly come to regret your decision for the rest of your life. And *I know* what that regret can feel like.

So choose.

If you're not prepared to open your mind to the potential in the world of crypto, then close up now. Burn this book, or delete it if you're reading a digital copy, and best of luck to you. Have fun trying your best but never being able to beat the elites at their own game. Have fun trying to build wealth and exist in a financial system that's designed for you to fight with one hand tied behind your back while others play with entire teams of the world's best.

Or are you with me?

Are you on board for what I believe will be the most exciting, exhilarating, risky and incredible ride you'll ever take in your financial life? Are you ready to consider your future, taking a punt on something new, breakthrough, revolutionary, and give yourself a chance to create a fortune that you would never have seen otherwise?

And I'm not just talking about a good chunk of money.

If this is as transformational and revolutionary as I predict, then we're talking about generational wealth. Wealth that could stand the test of time for centuries to come.

If you're ready for that journey, then buckle in. We're about to take you through everything you need to know about "crypto".

From the origins of Bitcoin and its importance through to the unique global environment of cryptocurrency, the initial coin offering (ICO) boom and the perceived "crypto winter".

There's a lot to cover. A lot to understand. Sometimes it's going to get a little technical. Sometimes a little dry – hopefully sometimes a little funny. But at the heart of it all, you need to continue to remember this is the beginning of something incredibly new and exciting. Something that's never existed before, and should be seen in its own right for what it is – not in direct comparison to the "traditional" concepts you might already know of.

I'm here to open your mind to the potential on offer should you embrace and immerse yourself in the world of crypto. To open your world to the revolution taking place. To *educate you*, make it simple for you, ease you into a world that you're unfamiliar with, maybe a little scared of and definitely interested about.

And by the end of it all if you're not absolutely convinced that there's an opportunity here for you, that's fine. Not everyone will see the opportunity.

But if you get even just one thing from all this, let it be the opening of the gate to a path that leads you into the world of crypto.

This could be the smartest and best decision *you'll ever make*.

So let's go. Let's take you through everything there is to know about crypto and the world you're about to step into.

And to do that we need to head into the past. We need to head back to the years before cryptocurrencies like Bitcoin, Ethereum, Litecoin or Ripple even existed.

It's important to understand the environment, the conditions and the mistakes of centralised authority to understand why cryptocurrency even exists.

You need to understand the past to understand the present. And then when you can understand the present, you will have a much better concept of what's coming in the future.

Chapter 2: Under the ruling thumb of central authority

The bubble burst. It wasn't even like the instantaneous explosion that you see in real time when you might pop a balloon with a pin.

It was the slow-motion version, the version captured on a 1,000+ frames per second slo-mo rig. You could see the moment the pin broke the surface tension. You could see the entire surface recoil and explode in all its glory. And then you were left with the sheer terror, realising that underneath it all was nothing but air.

It was brutal. It left scars that people still suffer from to this day. It was so vicious, so harsh that the toll wasn't even just financial; it even sparked the loss of human life. Nothing, absolutely nothing can capture how bad the 2008/2009 global debt crisis was. Nothing can be said except that the situation was avoidable. Every major financial crisis is avoidable – but there are common themes with every recent crisis. Often it's debt, greed and the thirst for power by centralised organisations, authorities and lawmakers.

But as bad as the debt crisis was, from the aftermath came a surge, actually more like a tidal wave, of growth and prosperity. But the question is, is it real prosperity? Is it real growth? Or is it the same old thing repackaged and played again?

We'll see when we look at this in more depth. But for all the devastation of the 2008/09 debt crisis, it certainly wasn't the first time the world had seen financial pain like this.

Just 10 years earlier the same thing happened. It was also an enormous event – albeit more specific to the technology industry. But this earlier crash in the 1990s was more like "the crash we needed to have".

For all the pain it created, it was the exact kind of crash needed to filter out the rubbish. It was exactly the medicine the market needed to let the strong, stable and genuinely revolutionary companies flourish – and flourish they did.

The tech bubble, or "dot-com" bubble, was one of the most devastating market crashes since Black Monday. And Black Monday had been the most devastating crash since Black Tuesday, 1929. And Black Tuesday had been the worst crash since... well, you get the point.

For as long as markets, central financial authorities, Wall Street elites, the global financially powerful, the "establishment" have existed, there have been market crashes. None of it the direct result of people other than those that sit in their ivory towers and determine the way the world turns.

But back to the dot-com bubble...

The 90s had seen an incredible surge in value of tech-related companies. It had seen indices like the Nasdaq rise from around 330 points in 1990 to over 5,000 points by March 2000.

That's an eye-watering 1,415% gain in a decade from an *index*! That's unheard of. Well it was unheard of until it happened. And of course it didn't continue. It all came crashing down as companies like Pets.com, InfoSpace, Kozmo.com and Boo.com went from being worth hundreds of millions or billions in some cases, to being worthless and shutting their doors.

They were the ultimate zero to hero to zero stories. And in a potential history repeating itself scenario, right now in the world of crypto something eerily similar might be happening... Read further on to see exactly what.

However, as bad as the dot-com crash was, from the ashes of the tech bubble of the 90s and early 2000s came companies like Google and Amazon. These companies were just cutting their teeth as tech companies, while others around them burnt to the ground. It would have been incredibly difficult times to build the companies they did. But they survived, and went on to become not just big tech companies but some of the most powerful organisations in the modern world.

The likes of Apple and Microsoft were alive well and

truly before the tech bubble. But they too survived. They dominated during the highs, and saw their stock plummet in the crash. It didn't kill them, though. They were too resilient. They had viable companies that were strong enough to make it through. It certainly shook them to their core, but they survived. And then they rose from the tech-bust ashes, and went on to dominate the world.

But the tech bubble, for all its glory and its destructive demise, was a necessary evil. And just like Black Monday in 1987 and Black Tuesday in 1929, the "tech wreck" left a lasting impression on the world, even to this day.

As we say, the tech bubble is something to take note of because it might just be a precursor to what we're currently seeing in the crypto world today. But not just for the ability to wipe out worthless tech companies, but also to let the strong survive and go on to dominate the world.

After the tech wreck the world markets were battered and bruised. While tech companies bore the brunt of the damage, other unrelated non-tech companies weren't spared either.

When markets tumble, investors typically take flight from *all stocks*, not just ones that might be directly impacted by the particular troubles of the moment.

Look at the FTSE 100 during the tech wreck. It went from a high of 6,930 points in late 1999 to a low of 3,490 by early 2003. The FTSE 250 had a similar fate. The Australian Stock Exchange All Ordinaries went from 3,425 points in June 2001 to 2,844 by September that year. And by 2003 was at 2,715.

That's even with an Aussie market practically sheltered from the tech wreck. Due to Australia being in the early stages of a huge commodities boom, it was almost untouchable for near on a decade. But the tech wreck was powerful enough to shake even that up a little.

And even the Nikkei 225 in Japan topped out at over 20,200 points in early 2000. By early 2003 it had been savaged to just 7,800 points. This was also because of the proportion of technology companies that existed in Japan.

Everywhere in the world felt the repercussions of the tech wreck. It made investing in tech companies a dirty idea. Well a dirty idea for some...

The smart money began to flood back to tech companies. Through the downward spiral and through into the recovery. Visionary investors could see that not every tech company was a dud. Some were diamonds in the rough. It became the dirty little secret that no investor talked about until a visible long-term recovery was under way.

After all, why would you invest in tech stocks after the carnage of 1999/2000?

But for those who had the capacity to see the forest through the trees, there was a smorgasbord of companies that would go on to reshape our future world. And those that invested early enough and at the right time were able to cash in on some of the most incredible gains ever seen on stock markets.

However, that all looked at risk (again) when 2008/2009 came around.

***

Now cast your mind back to 2008 and 2009. The tech wreck of 1999/2000 burnt down the house. But for the next eight years the house was rebuilt – supposedly bigger, stronger and fireproof.

But it wasn't. This house wasn't built of bricks. It wasn't built of sticks. It wasn't even built of straw. Heck, the reality was this wasn't even a house of cards.

This was a house built on the flimsiest of all material... debt. Packaged products, complicated, convoluted, confusing financial instruments that to this day most people simply don't understand. It was fake. It was money that never existed, "quality" assets that were junk. It was a house of nothing.

But this house won big. The house always wins remember? It saw incredible wealth – wealth that made fat-cat Wall Street bankers and fund managers filthy rich. And guess who was left holding the can when things really hit the fan? People like you, that's who.

While 1929, 1987 and 2000 were horrendous, 2008 was perhaps the worst of all.

It was simply one of the most significant financial events of all time. In fact, I'd go so far as to say it was one of the most pivotal events in the course of human history.

Not only did it shake financial markets to their knees, it also brought some of the world's biggest, most powerful nations back to earth. It crippled global budgets, destroyed global companies, left people broke, homeless – it ended up resulting in the loss of human life, such was the viciousness and devastating impact of the financial event most people know as the "global financial crisis" (GFC). For ease I'll continue to call it the GFC. But the truth is, it was a crisis of addiction to debt.

For decades prior, the world had been leveraging *everything*. While investors and companies leveraged up their portfolios and balance sheets, it was central banks and governments that were the worst offenders. In a boom time that would supposedly last forever, taking on debt was easy. Everyone was confident they could eventually pay it back. That's the idea of debt after all. And this new debt was used to build infrastructure, used to fund welfare, used to balance the budgets. It was the crack cocaine to a government junkie.

Government added debt to balance sheets in a way that had never been seen before. According to the Organisation for Economic Co-operation and Development, in 2000 the US general government debt was at 65.1% of GDP. The UK was 48.8%. Australia, 42.8%.

By 2008 the US general government debt was 93.1% of GDP. The UK was 63.4%. Australia 35.4% (we had a massive commodities boom, remember).

As I said, you think they'd have learnt that debt is not the answer. Even after 2008/09. But they didn't.

In 2016, the US government debt as a percentage of GDP was 127.5%. The UK was 123.1%. Even Australia's had climbed to 73.8%.

It's simply astonishing. But the scary part is it's showing no sign of slowing down. And if you think those countries are all bad – and they are – look at Japan.

In 2008 its general government debt to GDP was already 140.5%. By 2008 it was 178%. And by 2015 it was an eye-watering 234%.

Quite simply, over the last decade the world has gone broke.

Another way to think about it is if the world had to pay back every dollar of debt then the world would have – that's right kids – no money left. In fact, it'd owe money. But let's just call it a net zero. Broke and penniless.

Think about the enormity of that situation. Centuries... millennia of wealth built up over time. But over the course of a gluttonous, greedy, debt-addicted 20th century, the world is now effectively bankrupt. The world is the new "Lehman Brothers". *The world is worthless.*

Thanks to the complexities of global banking, the global financial and payments systems, through layers of debt, financial products and out-and-out confusion, banks and government around the world were able to load up with debt.

That is until some smart guys figured out that it was all ready to implode. And then it did.

The pinprick of the failure in the mortgage-backed securities (MBSs) market in the US saw a domino effect that had the US banking system spiral out of control.

Central banks around the world injected funds into the banking system, bailout money – taxpayer money – to save these banks. Some of them barely held on, such as Royal Bank of Scotland, AIG, Freddie Mac and Fannie Mae, and Merrill Lynch.

At one point the US Federal Reserve injected $236 billion in bailout money to the banking system. Bear Stearns received an emergency bailout from those funds.

It wasn't just the United States of America, though.

Citigroup had to inject £1 billion to bail out *six* of its own hedge funds.

By this stage Lehman Brothers in the US was on the verge of complete failure. It needed bailout money. But enough was enough. The Fed couldn't chip in any more; it was already up to its neck in it.

Merrill Lynch was in the same boat. But somehow through back room dealing, it was able to get a lifeline from Bank of America – which took them over.

Administrators from PriceWaterhouseCoopers had already dug their trenches at Lehman as things got worse. AIG was also in flames and burning up fast. From a split-adjusted price of around $1,450 per share in June 2007, by October 2008 AIG was trading at $34.

The head of the US Fed, Ben Bernanke, could handle Lehman's failing... just. But AIG was different. It was too big and too central to the US banking system. So in a nice display of playing favourites, once again the US dipped into its seemingly bottomless trust fund and pulled out another *US$86 billion* emergency loan to defibrillate AIG.

Things continued to deteriorate all over the world. "Bailout" was the new buzzword. Mainly because every government and every central bank in the world was looking at, if not already implementing, bailout packages to keep banks alive.

That money of course was taxpayer money. But if you remember 2008 at all – and you should – let us ask you this... did you get a say? Did they ask you if they could bail out the banks, or was it just something they did because they could?

Of course it was to protect investors and savers. The real risk was to your life savings. If these banks did fail, many people would simply lose life savings, investments, their entire livelihood. The worst part is that many did lose out big. Mum and dad investors, retirees, lost billions in the declining valuations of stock markets.

Plenty of people who worked in finance and banking were now already unemployed as banks began to immediately lay off staff and sell toxic assets to whoever would buy them... even though they were effectively worthless.

Investors and investments around the world were haemorrhaging money. Retirement savings of millions were in freefall. And the worst-case scenario was a real threat: that cash in the bank was also now at risk.

No financial market, no financial instrument anywhere was safe. Nothing. It was Armageddon. And then the US decided to implement the "Troubled Asset Relief Program" (TARP). This would, incredibly, buy the toxic assets of the banks, ridding them of the plague that had struck them down.

Only one problem: TARP was funded by taxpayer money.

The fact that TARP even existed is astonishing. Imagine going into a TV store and looking at all the nice new shiny TVs. Then in the corner is one that has a giant hole in the screen, no remote, severed power cord, and is effectively junk.

You wouldn't buy that TV would you? Well the US Fed would.

And it did. That was TARP.

Japan copped it in the neck, too. It was already in the midst of the "lost decade", when the entire 90s saw zero growth in the Japanese economy. It was now facing another "lost" decade, or two, or three. Maybe the Japanese economy would never see growth again.

Eventually a few banks merged and took over others. Some in Australia, the UK and Europe had enough capital backing that they were never in trouble of failure. And some of the real giants like Citigroup were able to ride out the storm.

But Lehman eventually filed for bankruptcy. At its peak in 2007 it was worth around US$60 billion in market cap. But it had US$639 billion in assets and US$619 billion in debt. It was the biggest bankruptcy filing in history, bigger than WorldCom, bigger than Enron.

"Too big to fail" became another term bandied about the world.

That's what the top-level execs at Lehman said prior to and during the crisis. They were wrong.

The aftermath resulted in global stock markets, the Nasdaq, FTSE, Hang Seng, Nikkei, ASX, all falling by around 50% and more. It smashed the value of investments and savings of people all over the world.

It destroyed any confidence in the global banking and finance system. And even now, nine years later, we're still feeling the effects of it. You'd think that the world's governments and central banks would have figured out that debt addiction was a road to nowhere. But they didn't.

But with all this going on, something truly beautiful was happening. A true revolution in global banking and finance.

Amongst all the turmoil of 2008/09, there was a groundswell in the digital world. A mysterious developer by the name of Satoshi Nakamoto released a white paper into the world titled *Bitcoin: A Peer-to-Peer Electronic Cash System*.

It wasn't long. Just nine pages in total (including references). But it would prove to be one of the most defining moments of the 21st century... that no one knew about.

The white paper and subsequent development of this idea would create **Bitcoin**.

But it was really only something that pure technologists, developers, hackers, purveyors of the "deep web", really knew about.

It was a fun, strangely exciting idea that a digital unit of exchange – separate from banks, government and financial institutions – could exist online.

It gained a small but loyal following. And with the aftermath of the financial crisis still in play, it was the perfect time for its arrival. It was anti-establishment. It was anti-bank, anti-financial institution. It was decentralised, anonymous, private – it was the financial instrument for the people. And it would become the most important financial development since the invention of "money" itself.

But it gained little attention to start with. It had no mainstream coverage. Most people had no idea about it, and the number of actual users tallied in the few thousand at best.

That is, until a number of key events (that I'll run you through later on) unfolded across the world over the course of the last seven years. Events which took Bitcoin from the realms of the deep web to the front pages of Bloomberg, Forbes and CNBC.

It would find its way into the discussions of the US Congress, Australia's Parliament, to the forefront of minds for investors, banks and financial institutions who had all been decisively caught asleep at the wheel.

As the financial crisis dissipated and the markets began to turn and recover in 2009, things seemed like they might all be right in the world again. But they were not. And over the next four years the centralised power across the world, central banks, governments, major financial institutions continued to perpetuate their addiction to debt... until 2013, when it all came to a head, again.

Chapter 3: Can we really be here again!?

2013. The world was again on the brink of financial collapse. Just four short years after the devastation of the 2008/2009 debt crisis. We had already seen markets plummet, investors lose trillions, people lose their homes, jobs, livelihoods, families and... lives.

Only now was the idea of recovery from the GFC starting to be a possibility. Even though many companies were still languishing at levels well below the peak of 2008.

The world was still feeling its way out of the GFC darkness. And the only way for government and central banks to deal with it was with more debt. Simply more and more and more debt.

And back in 2013, just four short years after the worst of the GFC had ended, the markets were again fearful of the inevitable, impending doom. Here we were *again,* teetering on the brink of financial Armageddon.

How on earth did we get here again? Was it something you said, something you did? Didn't you work hard enough? Didn't you save enough? Didn't you pay down your debts like a good boy or girl?

No, once again it had nothing to do with you. It was the excess, greed and addiction to debt that the world's governments hadn't been able to shake. They needed to go cold turkey. Instead they went back to their dealer, and asked for heroin this time instead of crystal meth.

But in 2013, while the world was still battling their debt addiction, much of the focus was on Greece and Cyprus. Greece was in the middle of their own government-debt crisis, which had seen radical change to the political landscape and major civil unrest. Unemployment levels were skyrocketing. In February 2013 unemployment hit 26.4% – the highest in the European Union. By April, youth unemployment was at an astonishing 60%.

Greece was looking like it couldn't repay its debts. Picture yourself in that position. What happens if you can't pay the debt on your home? Quite simply the banks take it off your hands.

If you can't pay, they take it away. And you're left with nothing, even though you've already forked out money to cover the repayments. When you can't pay your debt, you can also file for bankruptcy. That means you have to sell off all your stuff and pay back people you owe money to. But if the value of your stuff doesn't cover the debts, well bad luck to anyone who lent you money. They just don't get it back – they shouldn't have lent you money to start with, should they have?

So if a government can't pay its debts, it's a similar situation. It has to find a way to pay. That means selling off assets to raise money – often privatising major public industry. That means raiding the war chest... sometimes it might also mean raiding the financial institutions. Remember, the government can do as it pleases when push really comes to shove.

But still, if it can't pay it all back, if it doesn't have enough "stuff" to cover the debt, it goes bankrupt. It defaults. And anyone it owes money to doesn't get it all back.

Imagine if a country like Greece did that. Sure, it doesn't have a big economy. But if it can't pay its debt, then countries that lent it money don't get their money back. And that hurts them and their ability to repay other countries that they owe money to.

It's one big, scary downward spiral when countries begin to default on their debt. And Greece was on the brink of default. But even then, that was just the tip of the iceberg.

Cyprus was also going through its own financial crisis requiring an "emergency liquidity assistance" (ELA) programme from the European Central Bank (ECB). This was a bailout – just like the bailouts the banks received in 2008.

The idea was to prevent all-out collapse of the financial system in Cyprus. It had to do something because there was a "bank run". That means depositors were withdrawing all their money from the bank, based on the fear that the bank might become insolvent and take all their savings with it.

Heck, if I thought my bank was going to go under and take my life savings with it, I'd be doing the same. I'd be getting it out of that bank, out of the banking system and looking for somewhere else, <u>somewhere the banks or government couldn't get to it</u>... that is an important point.

There were people queuing up at ATMs trying to withdraw their money from the Cypriot banks. It became a mad rush, creating mania and hysteria, in order to get money out as fast as possible. The banks had to shut down their ATMs. They had to put a stop to withdrawals.

A bank run is bad because it becomes a self-fulfilling prophecy. When all the money goes, the bank has no deposits, no capital, no liquidity and no ability to stay alive. And they fail. And when they all fail, the system fails. And that spreads like a virus to other countries that held Cypriot debt. Or Greek debt.

If these two were to default, it would bleed out to the global banking system. Again, this would likely result in a systemic failure, which would probably result in another GFC.

It was an incredibly tense, albeit brief period where it really did look like GFC 2.0 would strike. It was looking like another banking system collapse in Europe, triggered by Cyprus, fuelled by Greece and then swiftly caught by the rest of the world.

This was all while countries like Iceland, Ireland, Italy and Spain were *still* reeling from the first GFC. And in the US its attempts to stave off another crash and crisis on home soil was resulting in levels of money printing by the US Fed like it was Monopoly money.

Just to make it all worse, earlier in 2013 the US had passed legislation called the American Taxpayer Relief Act of 2012 to try and avoid falling off the "fiscal cliff".

This was a potential situation where expiring tax cuts

and cuts to government spending would send the US into further economic decline, into a recession, and further damage an already broken-down system.

While it avoided the fiscal cliff, things weren't rosy for the US in 2013. The US government debt ceiling is a law created by US Congress. And in 2013 the debt ceiling was at US$16.4 trillion.

But in 2013 the US was on track to hit its debt ceiling. If it hit the ceiling then it would effectively shut down government. President Barack Obama made note it would not be able to pay wages to government employees, and the government would default on its obligations.

Obama and Ben Bernanke, (amazingly, still) chairman of the Federal Reserve, both pushed for the debt ceiling to rise to allow the government to continue to function. The debt ceiling did get a lift in May, to US$16.7 trillion. But they quickly approached it again.

Estimates were that around October/November the US government would stop paying its obligations and it too would default. And in case you don't remember, the US government actually went into partial shutdown mode on 1 October because it couldn't pay its bills or keep the figurative and literal lights on.

If the Greeks and Cypriots defaulting was going to be bad, imagine what it would be like if the US defaulted: KABOOM! Goodbye global finance, goodbye markets, goodbye "traditional" wealth. Again, this caused major concern amongst savers and investors, who were now getting desperate looking for alternative ways to store their wealth.

As you know, the US government is still functioning today, albeit barely. But its debt ceiling problem still lingers. And it'll continue to be plagued by it as long as it continues to see its debt obligations rise, and rise and rise. And a Donald Trump-led government isn't making it any better.

What's important to know is that in 2013 the world, the global financial system, was on the brink of Armageddon... again.

But as I said, in 2009 a financial phenomenon was taking the digital world by storm at the exact same time. And by 2013 it was starting to gather serious momentum. The conditions were again perfect for a surge in this revolutionary technology.

It was now far more known and accessible than it had been in 2009. It was new, risky, scary, complicated, exciting and revolutionary – it was an alternative financial instrument that was free from the turmoil of the global financial system. It was a haven outside of the reach and control of central banks and government.

Bitcoin was starting to thrive. And because of its design it was the perfect hedge against financial Armageddon in the "traditional" banking system.

It was unique, and by 2013 it was providing early-stage investors with gains in excess of 1,119,900% returns.

That's right – ***one million, one hundred and nineteen thousand, nine hundred per cent returns*** on their initial investment. Think that's mad? Well, it gets even crazier.

The world had seen nothing like it before. But the world was in a historic situation. A period of global financial instability that was unrivalled in history.

It was perfect conditions for Bitcoin to thrive.

Part of the reason that Bitcoin was becoming more recognised was the fact that it had seen such an incredible rise in price from its genesis.

In 2009 you could mine Bitcoin, get 50 "blocks" and at just a few cents per Bitcoin, you might be lucky enough to have those 50 Bitcoin be worth US$1. By 2010 those 50 Bitcoin would be worth $5, a 400% rise in your investment! Massive. Except by late 2013 at a price of US$1,120, those 50 Bitcoin were now worth US$56,000.

From a few cents to the price of an ounce of gold in the space of just three years. No wonder the world sat up and took notice!

In 2013 the world was dealing with major financial

troubles. But now the mainstream media began to pick up on the Bitcoin phenomena. It was and is the most disruptive, exciting financial development possibly in the history of banking and finance.

And in 2013 the world wanted to know more about this strange, exciting financial instrument by the name of Bitcoin. The turning point was when one Bitcoin was worth the same as the price of one ounce of gold.

As gold had and still is historically the investment of choice to hedge against financial calamity, sure enough serious "traditional" investors started to ask, what exactly is going on here? How can something seemingly worth nothing sell for the price of an ounce of gold?

It blew minds in the mainstream – it still does – and that's exciting. And the continued turmoil and trouble of global finance against the backdrop of an ever-increasing price of Bitcoin has sent its awareness globally into the stratosphere.

But from the tech wreck, the glory days of the 2000s, to the biggest financial collapse in history – the GFC – to the continued debt addiction, to the second coming of financial Armageddon in 2013, to the rising, and rising, and rising debt levels held by central banks and government, it's all created the perfect storm, the perfect environment, the perfect backdrop to the growth of Bitcoin. And this in turn has led to the subsequent growth of cryptocurrencies and the crypto economy.

But without these key moments of financial collapse and intervention, interference and meddling of the elite and the establishment, we would not have Bitcoin or cryptocurrency – well not likely.

Think about it – let's say that banks and government had practised responsible lending and prudent financial management for the last 100 years. Imagine they'd not created complex financial products to package up junk and sell it for massive profits, building a house of cards.

Imagine if there had been no financial crisis in 2009 because the banks had been good to customers, and hadn't tried to screw over one another and the population in order to beef up their multimillion-dollar bonuses.

Without the GFC, without the dot-com boom and bust, without Black Monday, there would be no Bitcoin, no crypto.

Yet here we are. Not only is Bitcoin worth multiple times as much as gold now, but it's also one of the most valuable, most desired (digital) assets in the world today. Its popularity is borderline hysterical.

The good news is that it's still early money, smart money that's now flowing to Bitcoin. The good news is if you're reading this, you're still early to the party, and that's a big opportunity.

When I speak to average people with little to no understanding of the world of finance and investment, they still have no idea about the "traditional" world of finance and even less idea about Bitcoin and cryptocurrency. But of the two they're far more excited and interested in Bitcoin and crypto than in the world run by the financial elites.

They know what money is, and they know that governments are drilling them to the wall. They don't like it. In fact many of them loathe the elite and the establishments that run their countries. But many of them don't know there's another way to go around it all. Many of them don't know about Bitcoin or its existence. But when we open their eyes to it, they want to know more. They want to get involved.

And as more people do learn about it and get involved, we see exponential growth ahead for its future.

The ironic thing about the rise of Bitcoin is it's the greed and excess of traditional banking and finance, of central banks and governments, that created the environment for all this.

Their hubris and greed helped to create new alternative financial instruments which will be the ultimate reason for their downfall. It's really a beautiful piece of poetry. The other irony is that now these massive financial institutions are wanting to get into "digital assets" and find a way to also ride the crypto revolution.

But another thing about it all is that most of the "establishment" can't see outside their own box of "traditional" wealth and greed. They don't understand the opportunity, they don't realise what's really at play. They don't see that the average man and woman, the "everyman", people like you, have a chance to become a part of this new, alternative financial system.

It's the ultimate libertarian movement, it goes around the greed and excess and gives everyone a chance to do something great. To take control of their own financial destiny and do it out of reach of all of those who stuffed it all up so badly for so many years.

So there it is, your history lesson on modern global financial calamity and the mess that it's become. This is an important foundation to understand as it lays the groundwork for the revolution we see today.

Remember, to truly understand why Bitcoin and crypto are so important, you have to understand the failures of the past.

The philosopher George Santayana said it best:

> *Those who cannot remember the past are condemned to repeat it.*

Chapter 4: The Key to Bitcoin is to understand the failures of the system

There's one more aspect of global banking and finance you need to get under your belt.

You see, to disrupt the existing system you need to also know how the *entire* current system works and why it's primed for disruption to begin with.

There's no future to Bitcoin if the current system works. If it's fair, efficient and works well, then what reason is there for Bitcoin to exist, to force change? There's none.

But the current financial and global payments system isn't efficient. It isn't fair. It isn't for the benefit of the many. It's skewed to favour the elite, the already wealthy; it doesn't give the average Joe and Jill a chance.

And when you break down the current payments system and understand how that works, then you see its deficiencies for all their glory. You see where it's broken, where it fails and the exact reasons why Bitcoin and cryptocurrencies are primed to disrupt the existing system and take it over.

To understand the current payments system you need to think about your own situation…

How do you get paid your wages today? It's pretty fair to assume you, like millions of other people around the world, simply see a number appear in your bank account each week, fortnight or month.

Your employer doesn't just pull you into their accounts department and hand over a wad of cash to you each month. Nor do they hand you an envelope with a cheque inside for your latest pay.

No. It's far simpler than that these days. I know that's how it works for me. I simply log on to my mobile banking app each fortnight and see if there's an extra supply of money in my account. If there is, then I've clearly been paid. If there isn't then I'm straight on the blower to accounts.

All we see is a number. We then typically use our online banking to shuffle that number around. Some people pay bills, some people send it to a savings account, some send it to another separate account for investment. Some go straight to the pub.

I have a routine where I shuffle my numbers around after each payday. Some goes to bills, some goes to savings, some goes to the day-to-day account and some goes to a currency exchange market.

This fortnightly shuffle of numbers can be a little disconcerting. For many people we're talking about thousands of dollars going through this "monetary ballet" from account to account, seamlessly and graciously flowing from left to right, right to left, spinning around jumping and leaping over here and there. Eventually it ends up in a final position where we applaud and cheer for the balletic money shuffle on display.

But at the end of the day, the way in which you receive and move your money around is purely digital. There's no physical handling of cash. The only time you typically ever actually see and feel "real" money is when you take it out of an ATM and use it to buy goods which you receive in your hands.

Let's get back to the point that today's money, the wages you receive, the income you generate, really are entirely digital already.

Let's say you have a daily account and a savings account with Bank A. You want to transfer between accounts. No problem. That's all done in house within the bank's internal systems. It never leaves the bank, it's just an internal shuffle. Simple.

Likewise, if you want to transfer $50 to your friend, Brad, who also has an account with Bank A. Again, it's all done with ease on Bank A's internal systems. It will simply debit and credit the figures from the accounts. Again, just an internal shuffle and the money never actually leaves the bank's internal system. Also simple.

Now let's say your friend Steve has accounts with Bank B. OK, so that's a little harder to do. Things now start to get a little more complex.

Bank A doesn't put your money in a sack and march it over to Bank B where it puts that money in a big safe. That's not safe or efficient. Sure that might have been the case before electricity, computers and connected systems. But that's not the world we live in today.

Instead Bank A reduces the amount from your account ($50) and then increases the amount in Steve's account with Bank B by $50. But how does it do this?

Bank A doesn't just have open access to Bank B's accounts. That would be a massive security and compliance risk. Instead, what happens is that Bank A and Bank B share an account with each other. It's like its own little lovely joint account. This shared account set-up is called "correspondent banking".

So Bank A decreases your account by $50. It increases its correspondent (joint) account with Bank B by $50. They it notifies Bank B with a message that the $50 now in their correspondent account needs to be allocated to Steve's account. By reconciling the message with their account, Bank B is happy to increase Steve's account. It can see the funds are there in their correspondent (joint) account.

This process is also relatively simple for banks and their existing network of systems. However even in "developed" countries, sometimes this bank-to-bank transfer can take a working day or two. Which really, in today's instant world, is inefficient and slow. In some countries however, this process is virtually instant, which is the way it should be.

The fact that banks can make it instant now is thanks to what's called a "deferred settlements" system. Effectively this just means they do their little balletic shuffling of money in and out and around the correspondent banking system, but they defer settlement until later in the day. They trust each other enough that the numbers match up, and they reconcile them later on.

Of course sometimes the numbers don't add up. That's

when fraud and theft departments start to stick their noses in and figure out what's going on. So even as big and as "trustworthy" as the banks might be, there's still plenty of fraud and theft occurring in the existing traditional banking and payments system.

But again, these are all domestic ways that banks shuffle your money around from you to other accounts for you, and through merchants, savers and investors.

When we start to go international, well things start to get really manic, really complex, even more inefficient and riskier.

Have you tried to transfer wealth across borders? Have you ever tried to send someone money overseas? Have you ever used your own debit or credit card in another country? Have you ever withdrawn cash from a foreign ATM? If you've answered yes to any of those questions, then you'll know that it can be hard to do.

For all the perceived advances in modern financial technology, the fact is that the system hasn't really changed since the 70s and 80s. Sure, you don't need to carry around travellers' cheques like you used to. And you don't need to withdraw wads of foreign currency before heading abroad. But the reality is it's no different. It's just digital versions of the same thing.

The banks still rip you off on exchange rates. They still take a cut of commission from your transactions. They charge you for using ATMs or even just making a purchase that isn't in the currency of your bank account.

They rip and steal funds from you at any chance they can get. But the problem isn't always necessarily your bank. They do sometimes have to charge you these fees, because they get charged these fees by other financial institutions, other intermediaries, middlemen and banks. They aren't going to just wear these costs, so they pass them on to you.

And this is where the whole system shows its true colours. They could all work together as a distributed network, making the whole system more efficient and streamlined. But they don't. They're all in it for isolated gain, to maximise returns to shareholders and investors.

They're simply there to profit from you. They don't really like you or care about you. You're an instrument in the existing traditional banking and payments system that lines their coffers, makes them billions in profits and pays for their huge bonuses. Without you they don't have a business. But if they could do what they do without you, they would.

Part of the reason that the entire international banking and payments system is so inefficient is thanks to the incumbent interbank organisation they call SWIFT.

The Society for Worldwide Interbank Financial Telecommunications is the global system that helps facilitate the shuffling of money around the world.

For example, if you want to send $1,000 from your account with Bank A to your cousin Rodney in the UK with Bank A-UK, you will need to provide a "SWIFT code" to ensure the transaction goes to the right bank and the right account.

What happens then is your Bank A sends a payment transfer SWIFT message to Bank A-UK. When this message arrive, clears and credits the account via their *correspondent banking* account, the process completes. This is time-consuming and can take days to complete, and can also be costly.

And this is even when the two banks party to the transaction actually hold correspondent bank accounts with each other.

But not every bank in the world holds a correspondent banking account with every other bank in the world. That means in order to get money from Bank A to Bank P in the Philippines, sometimes these payments have to go through financial intermediaries. These are middlemen that help in the processing and transfer of the payments – and they take their clip of fees on the way of course, which all adds to the complexity and cost of a transaction.

What's also important to know is that SWIFT doesn't actually send payments around the world. It never holds any actual funds. What it actually does is to facilitate payment and transaction *messages* (communications) between financial institutions to settle through correspondent accounts.

The actual movement of money is still all digital and between banks, financial institutions, middlemen and intermediaries.

Still with me? Good. This can get overwhelming. But stick with it because, as complex as this is, it's very important to understand how this complexity plays into the hand of Bitcoin and the future of Bitcoin so perfectly.

It's fair to say that the system we use now for local, domestic and international payments and money transfers is complex, can be expensive and is not easy once you leave one country, crossing a border to another.

And let's not forget that it's not just banks that facilitate payments. Sometimes you simply can't transfer money through the banks. This might be a situation where there's a person who doesn't even have a bank account.

So if you don't have a bank account how can you send money overseas, or even earn money?

Someone without a bank account probably sounds crazy to you, doesn't it? In developed countries it's very unusual for someone not to have a bank account. But according to the World Bank, approximately two billion people still don't have a bank account. That's roughly 27% of the world who still don't have access to the global banking and payments system.

The thing is these people still earn incomes and still work. The "shadow economy" is alive and well around the world. For example, a paper published by the Institute of Economic Affairs titled *The Shadow Economy* explains that the shadow economy makes up as much as 10% of GDP in the UK.

And if you look at the size of the global remittance market, you can further see that the transfer of funds around the world is only growing in size.

Transferwise, a peer-to-peer currency exchange platform, says:

In 2014 remittances to developing countries totalled a staggering $436 billion, out of a total of $583 billion worldwide.

What this tells us is that the bulk of international remittance goes from developed regions, US, UK, Europe to developing countries such as India, China, Philippines and Mexico. Transferwise also explains, "in 2012, migrants from China and India sent home a staggering $130 billion".

When it comes to the major players in the remittance market, companies like the US$9.10 billion payments giant Western Union [NYSE:WU] dominate the existing market.

But as I say, all of these ways to shuffle money around the world are complex and pass through many hands, adding incredible costs.

For example, again according to the World Bank, using banks to send money costs on average 10.96%. Using a money transfer company (like Western Union) costs on average 6.59%. And even using a post office costs 5.14%.

Across the three that's an average cost of 7.56% to send money around the world. Now if the total remittance market is about $583 billion, that's costs of $44.07 billion. $44.07billion that the global payments system rips from the hands of hard-working people just trying to make a living and make their way in the world.

I don't claim that the whole system should be seamless and free... or should it?

If you can cut out the middlemen and intermediaries, create a streamlined, simple, easy, borderless, decentralised system to shift money around the world, wouldn't that be a good thing?

In short, payments are hard. And SWIFT, which has allegedly improved the entire global payments system, has only been around since the late 70s. It's taken it 40 years working with banks and financial institutions, governments and central banks to create an incredibly complex web of payment infrastructure.

Without SWIFT there wouldn't have been a way to

move money around the world. And that's the problem. You don't have a choice. You want to send money, you must use the system that's been designed for you – and designed to benefit the elite.

We're all heavily reliant on these payments systems to shuffle money around the world. Without it, there hasn't been another way to shift your money about.

But what if there was another way?

Imagine a world with another choice. A choice external to the banks and financial institutions that simply rip people off. And what if we all moved to that new, alternative system? What if we moved because it was fairer, safer, faster and open to everyone on earth with little fuss?

What would happen to the incumbents in the banking system? How would the establishment look upon this threat to their billions in revenues and business? It's pretty clear that an existential threat to the banking, finance and payments system that's dominated the world for so long will not go down well with the heads of state and powerbrokers of the modern world.

It's fair to say they will fight any threat tooth and nail – unless they realise they can't fight it.

Instead, by conceding change is inevitable, they have a chance to pivot and become institutions that actually put their users first – which in itself would be the biggest change to the banking and payments system ever.

Well, the cryptocurrency ecosystem is a direct threat to the existing system. It's changing and evolving at such a rapid and ferocious pace that banks and financial institutions have no choice but to find a way in – otherwise they know that in the next 10, 20 or 100 years they'll simply become worthless.

However, these institutions still operate using fiat currency. That's currency issued by a centralised controlling entity, often a central bank and government.

So the US has the US dollar, the UK has the pound sterling, Europe (mainly) has the euro, China the yuan, and so on.

These central authorities are deeply entrenched in the existing global banking and finance system. They only know one way, their way.

They are only interested in their own currency, their own nation's wealth, they really only want to be more powerful, more wealthy and more dominant. They do this in the modern world through financial power. In the early parts of the 20th century they did it through military power. But today the dollar has more power than the bullet.

That's why, when the US wants to hurt Russia it doesn't go straight for the cruise missile shelf; it employs financial and trade sanctions on wealthy Russians, the Russian government and Russian companies.

It uses its financial clout as a weapon. It does this through currency intervention, manipulation and control. This is the currency war of the 21st century. And it's a war that's alive and well. But as nation states continue to play these currency wars, they lose the faith and trust of their citizens.

As they drive their economies into the ground putting up barriers and manipulate their currencies, they drive the people out to other alternatives. Previously people didn't have anywhere else to turn to. But now they do. And thanks to government meddling, they've contributed to the perfect storm that's allowing Bitcoin and cryptocurrency to flourish.

Thanks to the incompetency of governments, central banks and the existing global banking, finance and payments system, the people of the world, the average Joe and Jill, now have another way to succeed and flourish financially in the world.

Chapter 5: The dark web and FOMO

Now you know the system inside out, the failures of the past and its problems. You know the world which gave birth to Bitcoin.

And there's no disputing that Bitcoin was "the first" meaningful crypto. Without Bitcoin there are no others. Its importance cannot be overestimated. But will it be the most important in the future? We'll see. It will play a role, as will other cryptos. And, in my view, it will be worth considerably more in the future than it is even today.

But now you understand the world in which Bitcoin started, you need to know about Bitcoin itself. Why is it even a "thing"? Why is it worth so much money – in terms of fiat money that is? Why does it continue to carry such incredible valuations – after all, if you subscribe to "traditional" thinking it has no backing, it's a purely digital instrument, and that makes it worthless, right?

Wrong.

Kitco is one of the world's premier sites for market commentary, live spot prices and retail access to gold and other precious metals.

But in 2013 even Kitco news put out an article that was plastered everywhere from its own website to *Forbes*, declaring, "2013: Year of the Bitcoin".

Why on earth would a gold and precious metals website proclaim 2013 to be "Year of the Bitcoin"? Well for many mainstream pundits, Bitcoin is also known as digital gold.

It carries many similar properties to gold...

There is a finite amount of gold in the world. There is a finite supply of Bitcoin that will ever be in existence.

To get physical gold (without just buying it) you have to mine it from the ground using specialised mining equipment. To get Bitcoin (without just buying it) you have to mine it by solving an algorithm using specialised computer equipment.

And, of course, you can just buy both if you wanted to.

In times of financial turmoil, gold tends to perform well. In times of financial turmoil, Bitcoin tends to perform extraordinarily – OK, slight difference there.

The point is that to many pundits, Bitcoin is digital gold. And it's a reasonable argument. In fact, in its current form, Bitcoin is more like an asset than it is a true currency. And I'll explain that idea as I get a little more technical on Bitcoin.

But the most glaringly obvious difference between gold and Bitcoin is you can touch and feel gold. There's nothing physical about Bitcoin. It's a completely online, digital asset.

That makes is hard for some people to comprehend, but it's what also makes it so incredibly unique – it's what makes it like nothing else before, a whole new asset class.

Back in 2013 this online digital "currency", as people were also referring to it, had become one of the most outstanding investment performers in the history of investing.

On 31 December 2012 one single Bitcoin was worth the equivalent of US$13.51. On 4 December, 2013, one Bitcoin was worth US$1,147.25. And by June 2017 that Bitcoin was worth over US$3,000.

That's a return from 2012 to 2013 of 8,391%. And from 2012 to 2017 of 22,105%. Nothing else in the world has ever provided a return that significant in such a short space of time.

But that wasn't even the beginning of it. For early owners of Bitcoin the returns by December 2013 were actually in the *millions of per cent.* In fact in October 2010, if you had been in the know, you could have secured Bitcoin for just 10 US cents.

Imagine that. Picking up 1,000 Bitcoins for just US$100. And then in around seven years seeing that US$100 stake turn into US$3 million.

The maths is easy to do. That's a 2,999,900% return on investment.

Quite simply *nothing else in history* has done that well. And perhaps, more importantly, nothing on earth has ever continued to exist at such high levels, at that kind of world-changing growth.

Even today Bitcoin remains steadily over US$2,500 per Bitcoin.

The question on the lips of the world is, how? The smartest minds in finance simply don't get it. I know world-class bankers and economists that I have to walk through this step by step with a guiding hand.

It's incomprehensible to them that this even exists, let alone has the power to change their world and challenge the very existence of the companies they work for, worth hundreds of billions of dollars.

How does a "digital currency" really go from nothing, from complete obscurity, to a legitimate financial instrument in the space of just seven years? How can nothing, and I mean literally nothing but computer code and algorithms, become worth around US$100 billion based on current circulation and prices?

We could also ask how a couple of guys making computer boards in a garage could go on to create the world's largest consumer device company, worth US$900 billion in just over 41 years.

How do a couple of guys developing operating system software for "personal computers" go from nothing to a company worth US$970 billion in just 42 years?

These are two examples of (combined) US$1.87 trillion worth of market capitalisation that were started from nothing.

People didn't understand Apple or Microsoft when they started. Even up until the turn of the century, people still doubted whether Apple would ultimately succeed. People doubted Bill Gates and Paul Allen. They doubted Steve Jobs and Steve Wozniak.

The establishment thought they knew better. The incumbents thought they couldn't be dethroned. But they were. And if these are just two examples of creating over US$1 trillion worth of value from nothing in just over 40 years, imagine what crypto can do.

Imagine what's possible now with the technology available. What's possible with a disruptive, revolutionary financial ecosystem that's taking on the establishment, taking on the incumbents.

Imagine being able to invest in Microsoft or Apple in 1980. Well that's the kind of opportunity I'm talking about with Bitcoin and crypto – except it could be bigger.

If Bitcoin held a total circulation value now of US$970 billion and Ethereum (which I'll get to later) was $900 billion, they would be worth 7.76 times and 45 times more than they are now.

That would put Bitcoin at US$54,940 and Ethereum at US$8,505. The risk here isn't about losing your investment if you decide to get involved in crypto (although that is a real risk you should be aware of). The way I see it the biggest risk is *not taking an opportunity, doing nothing* and missing out on the potential to change your financial life.

And it's this <u>fear of missing out</u> (FOMO) which is driving many of the gains in all cryptocurrency and Bitcoin right now. Normally that would concern us – if I were talking about traditional stocks and other financial products. But I'm not.

When it comes to Bitcoin and Ethereum a bit of FOMO is good for the cause. But when it comes to other crypto, new ICOs and what I like to call "crapcoins" or "trashcoins", well, FOMO takes on a whole different tone.

However, this is still early days. So FOMO with Bitcoin and Ethereum is limited to those who understand the long-term potential on offer here. FOMO for trashcoins is pure greed and speculation, wanting to find returns like the millions of per cent that Bitcoin saw in the last 10 years –

and *that* is a worry.

But with crypto that has genuine network value (a concept I'll explain later) it's just smart money going to where the opportunity lies.

FOMO does also worry those thinking about getting into crypto but yet to pull the trigger. Even you might be thinking that FOMO is a risk to the price of Bitcoin or Ethereum right now.

So let's dispel that idea.

FOMO is a bizarre acronym. You might have seen it on social media previously. One of the "kids" posting #FOMO on their Snapchat, Instagram or Twitter account. Heck, I've used the #FOMO on Twitter before – and I'm by no means one of the "cool kids".

You might have just casually come across it in conversation but never realised. Believe it or not, FOMO is a legitimate psychological condition. And it's never been as prevalent as it has been since the turn of the century.

With the rise in social media (Twitter, Facebook, Snapchat, Instagram, LinkedIn) the human condition has evolved to all new levels of stress and anxiety.

A research paper in 2016 from the Journal of Business & Economics Research, *Social Media and the Fear of Missing Out (Volume 14, Number 1 – Abel, Buff, Burr)*, highlights the link between social media and FOMO:

> *Social media sites play an essential role in the fear of missing out. While it is possible that FOMO has existed for as long as communication channels have existed, there is no doubt that social media's presence in our lives has amplified the need and desire (and opportunity) to know what other people are doing and saying at all times.*

We live in a world of instant communication. A world where social media and 24/7 news content is in our face all the time. It results in a condition where people are sensitive to the idea that perhaps somewhere, someone else is doing something more fun, exciting, just simply better than what they're doing at any given moment.

It's why people wake up in the morning and the first thing they do is trawl through their social media threads. They want to see and know what everyone else is doing. They want to feel a part of something better. They want to know that what they are doing or about to do is as exciting as what others might be doing – and they want others to know it.

It's a world that perpetuates its own narcissism and vanity simply through the fact of FOMO.

And it's this FOMO that also drives people to act and behave erratically. It's what causes internet articles, videos, blog posts, pictures and comments to go "viral". It's an all-immersive world where people want to share and connect in the digital world and display the successes or perceived successes they might achieve.

So when in 2013 when Bitcoin initially took off in notoriety and price, it's fair to say that the idea of Bitcoin and the mystique of Bitcoin connected at the perfect time as social media was becoming truly all-pervasive. And it then attracted a lot of people suffering from FOMO.

At the time, it seemed an artificial inflation of price. And when the price crashed it appeared that was indeed the case. But hindsight tells us that perhaps FOMO wasn't such a bad thing then. FOMO can also "spread the good word", and in this case the good word was Bitcoin.

The FOMO of 2013 helped fuel an already raging fire, as people saw other people buying Bitcoin and making a bundle of cash along the way.

Not wanting to miss out on this incredible story saw more people pile in. And as it all went viral, even for a short time, FOMO took hold, and the digital world piled in to this digital currency. It too became a self-fulfilling prophecy. And the price went up... and up... and up... and up, to that incredible milestone of a one million per cent gain in price.

But as I say, the FOMO of the social media world was just the beginning. As news outlets took hold of this incredible story, it hit the headlines worldwide. Forbes, Bloomberg, BBC and Reuters – every single major news agency in the world was reporting on the incredible rise of Bitcoin.

It was global FOMO.

This saw forward-thinking "investors" sit up and take notice. All of a sudden this mysterious, underground, deep web digital "currency" was front-page news *worldwide*. This only added to the hype and hysteria. And away it went again.

This was all fuel to a raging fire, as I explained earlier. Which leaves the question, what sparked the raging fire to begin with? If FOMO fuelled it, what started it?

And that all boils down to a secretive online marketplace for drugs, guns, hitmen and fake IDs...

This was an online marketplace where you could buy and sell illegal items. But easily the most popular goods for sale were drugs. Weed, hashish, ecstasy, MDMA, cocaine, heroin... whatever your poison, it was available.

Unlike dialling up a dealer and having to deal face-to-face with a criminal, people could simply jump on to their computer, order some Class A narcotics and have it sent to them via a dead drop location (if they were smart).

They could do it all online and, importantly, with no paper trail and, at the time, 100% anonymously. Imagine that. Unfettered access to any drug you could think of, and the authorities had *no idea this was going on* right under their noses – at least in the early days.

An illegal community existed online where people could freely buy and sell illegal goods and services. It was all done with complete anonymity and safety, and there was no monetary trail to follow.

It was the perfect, no, the ultimate system for nefarious characters to operate. And it was real. We saw it. We didn't buy from it, but it would have been easy. This market existed on the deep web. Its name, Silk Road.

It was in effect the ultimate black market in the deep, dark parts of the internet that most people didn't even know (and didn't want to know) existed. And the thing people most wanted to know was, how could they get away with it?

But what is this "deep web"?

The deep web is the parts of the internet you've never seen. It's the bigger part of the internet, the uncatalogued part, the part you don't want to know about and don't want to visit.

It's a place online where websites can exist under the radar, unknown to the masses. Often it's run through a TOR network. That's an "onion router" network.

Picture an onion. Cut it open. Peel back the first layer, what do you get beneath? More layers. This layering is the framework on which the deep web is built. You can go through one layer, only to find another layer and another and another. Meanwhile the IP address is bounced from server to server around the world.

It's virtually impossible to find and track down. And sites change location all the time so as to not be found and shut down by the authorities. And even when these kinds of sites are found, two more spring up in their place. It's this kind of growth and evolution of the deep web that's made it far bigger than people realise.

Estimates are the "visible web", the web you see through Google or Bing, is around 4% of the information available on the internet. The remaining 96% exists in the deep web.

It's hard to track, nearly impossible to index. But it exists. It's deep, it's dark. It's incredible really. At around 500 times the size of the surface web, the deep web is the perfect location to hide an illegal drugs and firearms website.

Mind blown yet?

But what makes the deep web and in particular the Silk Road so fascinating was the ability for it to be anonymous and virtually untraceable. That realisation that someone can go online, buy drugs and have no money trail was astounding in the modern world – but not unexpected.

Most people couldn't get their head around the fact this site could operate as a market yet with no financial institution, no kind of account or "traditional" payment methods (like cash) attached in order to pay for the drugs and guns.

To buy and sell on the Silk Road, users paid and received "currency" in Bitcoin.

While many people assume one of the earliest exchanges of Bitcoin for goods was for a couple of pizzas, the reality is it was more likely for drugs and guns in the deep web. But we'll never know for sure. And that was the appeal of Bitcoin on the Silk Road in the deep web. No one was sure of anyone or anything. The only thing known for sure was that a mysterious operator by the handle "Dread Pirate Roberts" was the main administrator of the site.

It was the ultimate trust-less system, it was the ultimate trust-less currency. There was no bank, no bank account. It was a cryptographic token exchanged from an anonymous wallet address, sent to another anonymous wallet address. Then goods were sent to an anonymous user at an anonymous location working off a computer that could exist in Lithuania one minute, the US the next minute, Germany, Bolivia, the Czech Republic, Bermuda and Kazakhstan, all within the space of minutes.

In the early days, around 2010 and 2011, Silk Road was the poster child for everything the establishment hated about Bitcoin. It still kind of is today as well.

Once authorities got wind of Silk Road, they decided very quickly it was bad news.

Due to its unique property of anonymity (at the time) Bitcoin was clearly the obvious choice for criminal exchange on Silk Road. But don't forget, before Bitcoin, cash was the king of the criminal world. So for every negative aspect of Bitcoin being the currency of choice for bad actors, just remember cash did the same thing before it – and no one seems to have an issue with cash.

Silk Road was an incredible, revolutionary operation. Sure it was illegal, but its very existence helped to fuel the rise of Bitcoin from the deep web into the public consciousness.

It was a salacious story. A mysterious part of the internet, 500 times bigger than what most people realised. A dark, secretive website where anyone could buy drugs and guns from the comfort of their computer. And the unit of exchange underpinning it all, fuelling the fire and making the criminals wealthy, was a new, mysterious digital currency called Bitcoin.

You couldn't write a better script if you were trying to make a blockbuster Hollywood movie. And even Hollywood movies on crypto don't even come close to the thrill of the real-life events.

But for those operating in the deep web and on Silk Road you had access to drugs, guns, fake IDs, human trafficking, hitmen... and worse. It was all there for sale on the "deep web". And the primary "money" flowing between the buyers and sellers was Bitcoin – all because it helped the buyer and seller operate commerce with complete anonymity.

By the time Bitcoin began to hit its incredible price highs in 2013 it was well known amongst the deep web community and forums all over the deep web and "surface net" were buzzing about Bitcoin. By 2013, Silk Road had been in operation for two years. It had already made a lot of criminals wealthy. And it had done so accidentally. If it cost $100 for a gram of cocaine in 2011, in terms of Bitcoin that would have been anywhere from 100 to 5 Bitcoins.

For a drug dealer who received 100 Bitcoins in 2011 and held on to those proceeds, by 2013 that would have been worth $100,000 – or 1 kilogram of cocaine. You can start to figure out now just how this drew the ire of authorities – for once, they weren't making all the money and they couldn't control this network.

The development of Silk Road actually started around August 2010. At that point in time one Bitcoin was worth just 7 US cents, and a gram of cocaine would have set you back (based on a $100 price) 1,428 Bitcoins! Fortunately for buyers of drugs, the Silk Road user site didn't officially launch until February of 2011.

By then the price of one Bitcoin had already increased more than 1,328% to reach the lofty heights of US$1! So those Bitcoins could buy a lot more drugs than they could have done just six months earlier – a great moment for buyers!

Much of this was going on under the noses of everyone, it was a very secretive and clandestine operation. Until 1 June 2011.

It was on this date one of the most significant news articles in the history of Bitcoin was published on the website Gawker, by the author, Adrian Chen. The title of the piece was, *The Underground Website Where You Can Buy Any Drug Imaginable.*

The article was an op-ed piece about Silk Road. That was the main focus. But it was the other detail, the new, crazy "currency" in the article, which really caught everyone's attention. Chen uses a real-world example of how easy it was to buy drugs on Silk Road:

> *Mark, a software developer, had ordered the 100 micrograms of acid through a listing on the online marketplace Silk Road. He found a seller with lots of good feedback who seemed to know what they were talking about, added the acid to his digital shopping cart and hit "check out." He entered his address and paid the seller 50 Bitcoins – untraceable digital currency – worth around $150. Four days later the drugs, sent from Canada, arrived at his house.*

The article on Gawker went viral. It became one of the most talked about articles of 2011 amongst the "tech head" forums around the net. It received coverage on a few major news sites, but the mainstream was still oblivious to what was going on.

The deep web community was up in arms about the uncovering of the Silk Road, but the thing that really ended up capturing the imagination of the wider community was this "untraceable digital currency", Bitcoin. It instantly grabbed the attention of technologists and futurists as many quickly came to realise that this was the early stages of something serious, something transformative, something disruptive – something with the potential to completely revolutionise the entire global financial system long term.

What was even more insane about Bitcoin was the fact that it was an accepted form of "money" in the digital world that you could actually use to buy things and receive payment for things. And it was untraceable (at the time). If you wanted you could convert it back into fiat currency, dollars and pounds. And you could mine it – in other words, you could create it yourself out of thin air.

While not the idea or central premise of Bitcoin, the attractiveness to make some quick cash was all too tempting.

And then just to top things off, it was the impossible made possible...

As a child your parents often tell you that "money doesn't grow on trees". This usually comes after you plead for a few bucks to buy something you really want. And as a life lesson they tell you, no, money doesn't grow on trees. Well technically they were correct. That is until Bitcoin came along.

Bitcoin allowed users with the right technical proficiency and the right computer equipment to rip that money off the money tree. It was the ability to be your own royal mint, to print your own money.

From the very beginning you could mine Bitcoin, that's part of its technical design. Your reward for mining, which really means solving its algorithm using a computer, was blocks of Bitcoin. And as each Bitcoin was worth real fiat money, each block was worth *something*.

People began to realise this in fact was the mythical "money tree". You could mine Bitcoin from nothing and instantly by doing this you would have something that was worth real money.

These early days held incredible parallels to the great Gold Rush era. Those in the know flooded to this "digital gold" and things got a little crazy.

When Chen published the article about Silk Road on Gawker, Bitcoin was trading at US$9.21. After hitting US$1 in February, and with the growth of the Silk Road and the deep web awareness of Bitcoin, it had increased a further 821%.

But just 10 days after the release of Chen's article, the price of Bitcoin hit US$17.61. That's a 1,661% rise from February and an incredible 25,057% from August 2010.

In just 10 months the price of one Bitcoin had gone up 25,057%. This was the first massive run for Bitcoin. With such a short history it had become a cult hero in the digital world. It had all the hallmarks of the perfect financial instrument for anarchists, libertarians, anti-establishment movements – it was the ultimate disruption to global finance, arriving at a time when people wanted nothing more than to "stick it to the man".

But its early meteoric rise didn't last.

By the end of 2011 one Bitcoin was again just worth a couple of dollars. Also its rise to incredible price highs, its infamy thanks to Chen's article and its clear links with the illegal online world had already begun to put it on the radar for the authorities and lawmakers.

While the Gawker article was crucial in the growth of Bitcoin, it also hamstrung it, at least for a short time. When you look back at the influence of that article at that time it really served two purposes...

1. It brought the world of the deep web and illegal activity and Bitcoin to technologists and futurists.

2. It brought the world of the deep web and illegal activity and Bitcoin to law enforcement and the authorities.

For all its promise and hope, Bitcoin was also creating enemies. And you can guess where those enemies were coming from. Government, lawmakers, centralised authority, all those that Bitcoin challenged, wanted to end it.

Bitcoin equates to change. It is so disruptive, such a revolutionary change, that the power of the elite and the establishment wanted nothing more than to quash it.

And for all of 2012 it seemed like they were having their way. In 2012 Bitcoin floundered. Many people believed it was dead on arrival. It would falter and fail before it ever really took off. And all indications were that it would probably remain a niche online unit of exchange for geeks, nerds, and the complicated and complex world of the deep web.

But they were wrong. As we know, while 2012 might have been a year of uncertainty for Bitcoin, this was the financial instrument of the people. And nothing was going to stop it now. Its rise from 2009 to 2010 and into 2011 was incredible. Its fall and perceived demise in 2012 was nothing more than a speed bump.

We know this because 2013 happened. And as we know, it became "The Year of the Bitcoin" – and the year that Bitcoin went from obscurity to a viable, legitimate and ultimately powerful revolution.

However, by 2013 the really early movers had already made their mark. The deep web and Silk Road brought attention – and then the FOMO really kicked in.

This wouldn't be the first time we'd see immense FOMO kick into crypto markets. And it wouldn't be the biggest FOMO run we'd seen. That title would go to the 2017/18 explosion.

But in 2013 it's important to recognise what really triggered the bull run. You see, the global environment always plays a big hand in how Bitcoin and crypto performs. It's fair to say that crisis is the friend of crypto.

Chapter 6: Crisis: crypto's best friend

Remember our earlier talk about the Greek financial system and almost-collapse back in 2013, which sent Bitcoin prices skyrocketing?

Well, Greece is now one of many countries again on the brink of defaulting on its government debts. The country could once again be looking at financial Armageddon, another major run on the banks.

There's even talk from ministers in the Greek government about dropping their currency (the euro) and resorting to the US dollar as their currency of choice. That's one of the wildest currency plays we've seen in the last couple of years... or is it?

We're also seeing some of the most volatile, explosive, wealth-eroding bickering between two of the world's great superpowers: the US and China.

Meanwhile, the Eurozone is heading towards recession, and maybe even depression should things get really bad. Add to the mix a political mess in the UK, Asia crumbling under extensive debt because of China's Belt and Road Initiative and parts of South America falling into absolute chaos.

Outside of wartime periods, I can't recall there being a more volatile and crisis-laden world.

All of this is part of the reason for the continuing strength in the growth of cryptocurrencies.

Now, we know with a failed system and crisis after crisis in the early part of the 21st century that the environment was ripe for Bitcoin to flourish. We know that the failings of government and central banks around 2008 and 2009 helped to make this alternative financial system a haven for people who simply had nowhere else to turn to keep their wealth out of the grubby hands of the establishment.

But today what's happening in the world is going to fuel that fire even more. The failings of central banks and the instability and extraordinary actions of governments are simply destroying wealth in countries across the world. With people now aware of alternative stores of wealth like Bitcoin, there's a huge power shift out of the traditional systems and into the new crypto economy.

And when you have a clearer understanding of the difficulties of the payments system and the world's manipulated and corrupt currencies, then you'll be able to understand why Bitcoin is the solution to the world's problems. And the biggest opportunity in finance that has ever existed.

Currency woes

For example, when I have a dollar and I want to take that and buy another currency, say British pounds, I have to exchange it.

That means I sell my dollar into a currency market where another party will buy it from me using pounds at a rate that the market decides is fair. For example, say one Australian dollar is worth around 0.6 British pounds.

I get 55 pence for my Australian dollar – except there's one caveat on that exchange rate. That's the *wholesale* exchange rate. In reality, if I'm exchanging my Aussie money using my retail bank and I want to buy British pounds and I sell my dollars to my bank, who give me pounds in return, I'm using the bank's *retail exchange rates*. This means added fees and commissions, and I end up with far less than the wholesale rate.

For example, the Aussie Bank retail rate might be just 0.51 British pounds for my Aussie dollar. That's a 7.8% difference between the wholesale rate and the retail rate. In other words, 7.8% is what the bank makes just for the courtesy. Sound fair? Not really.

That's bad enough as it is. But then there's also the meddling of the central banks of Australia (Reserve Bank of Australia, RBA) and the UK (Bank of England, BoE), who can push those rates wider apart or closer together. A shift in interest rates from the RBA or BoE can swing a currency wildly up and down. Either way, someone on one side of the trade loses out at the influence of the central bank and political policy.

To give you an idea, historically one Aussie dollar has got as little as 30 British pence and as high as 70 British pence. Now that kind of international currency fluctuation is solely the result of the influence of centralised power. I never get to influence how that changes, it's all at the hands of the establishment, the financial elites.

This is just one aspect of the difficulty and added expense of exchanging currency from one country to another country. While it might be easy to travel around the world now, it's incredibly difficult to get your money anywhere outside of the place you live – and there's something very wrong about that.

But there's more to currency than most people appreciate. And perhaps the most significant factor influencing currencies is the actual exchange rate itself.

A country's currency value is dependent on supply and demand factors from international money markets. The supply and demand is influenced by a range of economic factors. For instance, the value of the Australian dollar and its supply and demand is influenced by factors including:

- The cash rate set by RBA.

- Imports and exports.

- Economic growth (or lack thereof).

- Other countries' cash rates and whether they are high, low, moving up or moving down.

- The volume and speed of money flow through an economy.

- Other countries demand (or lack thereof) for Australian exports.

- Overall economic stability.

- Political stability.

- Banking system stability.

- Debt that a country holds or issues to and from other countries.

Most significantly, however, is the ability for a country to manipulate its currency by getting its central bank to move the cash rate. These influencers are typical of a free-float currency like the Aussie dollar, US dollar or British pound.

However, some currencies (and Australia's used to be like this, prior to December 1983) are determined using a reference rate, which the country's central bank determines. And sometimes, as in the case of China, they can overnight decide to change that reference rate to sharply devalue or appreciate the value of their currency to suit their needs.

This can, has, and will play havoc on international currency markets. But it also plays havoc on the wealth of citizens. Imagine your cash savings were effectively worth 20% less overnight, should a government decide to manipulate the currency lower just to correct the balance of payments they stuffed up to start with?

In fact this, combined with currency manipulation such as the quantitative easing (money printing) programmes from the US and interest rate hikes or cuts used by some of the world's major central banks (US Fed, British BoE, Australia's RBA), all leads to a currency market in the grip of extreme turmoil. Some astute financial minds even call it all-out currency wars.

Back in 2017 there were currency wars playing out all over the world because of the difficulties of the global banking system, piles and piles of government, household and corporate debt and because of trade, military, political and economic tensions between many of the world's countries.

For example, President Trump is seemingly making a game of how many new political enemies he can create while in office. He's single-handedly turning governments who were once allies against him.

But he's also promised to go on a major spending binge in the US. He wants to spend billions on new infrastructure projects to rebuild US roads, bridges, railroads and everything else he possibly can.

And let's not forget about the "wall". You know that big 'ol concrete wall dividing the border of the US and Mexico? That wall that Trump promised he would get started on right away, that's still in the planning phase.

Well this is all grand, but the problem he faces and the problem that's facing the US dollar is how the heck is he going to pay for it all? There's one solution to this problem: Debt.

It's a similar situation in the UK with policy that wants to re-nationalise major infrastructure and services. This is all fine in theory, but this all comes at a cost, and that cost has to be borne by someone – the taxpayer – or also a combination of, debt.

Excessive debt leads to a weaker economy. It might provide short-term relief, but we all know where it ultimately leads. It leads to problems with currency, problems with the economy, problems with growth, wages growth, inflation – just a lot of problems stacking debt on debt.

Eventually, you find that the debt piles up so much like in the US that new money printing and bond issuance is really just to pay the interest costs on the debt already incurred. It's debt to fund debt. And we all know how that ends up.

In the UK, things are equally balanced on a knife's edge. The Tory government is in shambles unable to deliver the Brexit that the referendum promised. The Labour Party also can't put together any semblance of a plan forward, and now you're seeing immense growth in popularity from the Brexit Party simply to deliver to the British public something that democracy was supposed to have delivered.

The UK is a prime example of democracy failing. And as people start to realise (finally) that politicians and centralised authority don't really care about them or their well-being, then society is starting to turn the tide against power and look for alternative means of looking after themselves.

EU powerbrokers must have been laughing all night long during the UK election and the process towards a Brexit, which at the time of writing still hasn't happened.

I don't think the EU no longer cares about it all, it wants to punish Britain. It stems from the fact that Britain never really committed to the relationship from the start. Remember, the UK never actually adopted the euro as its currency although it became a member of the European Economic Community (as it was called then, now the European Union) back in 1973. Britain retained the pound sterling – which was probably the best decision it ever made regarding Europe.

But even with the UK leaving the EU, there are now concerns over inflation, trade and tariffs, trade agreements, immigration and political instability. All making the pound head sharply lower, making it weaker against other currencies on historic levels.

The worry is that Brexit, whenever it happens, is going to cripple the UK. Maybe it will, maybe it's a lot of fearmongering. But to the average person, their wealth and their way of life is at stake. And that's a risk that terrifies the average person.

But again, while the EU may be enjoying watching the UK squirm, it's got its own problems and demons to face.

Thanks to the UK leaving the EU and the rise of right-wing political parties across Europe, it's looking like others might join in and hand in their EU memberships.

The Netherlands' elections saw an upsurge in popularity from far-right parties. Their most controversial politician is the right-wing, anti-Muslim immigration, Geert Wilders and his Party for Freedom. While the party didn't win the Dutch elections, it saw a rise in popularity.

And it's not going away in a hurry.

Perhaps in the next set of Dutch elections Wilders and the Party for Freedom will win the vote in the Netherlands.

If he does, then we could be looking at the Netherlands also leaving the EU – and possibly going back to its own original currency, the Dutch guilder.

In Austria the country narrowly avoided the far-right wing Freedom Party of Austria in elections late 2016. In a similar situation to the Dutch, the far-right was beaten, but battled on after gaining significant numbers of votes over their campaign.

Then in snap legislative elections in 2017 it didn't win the vote but entered parliament under a coalition with the leading party.

Perhaps in the next Austrian elections, the Freedom Party of Austria will gain an absolute majority and outright leadership.

France has also recently seen out an election. This was perhaps the most significant election in 2017. It threw up the same kind of emotive response from the world as the Trump/Clinton elections in the US.

France and Germany are the two most central and powerful nations that make up the current EU. Luckily for the EU, Emmanuel Macron was successful in his campaign. But it was his opposition that again continues this trend in Europe of anti-establishment, right-wing, anti-EU parties strengthening.

Marine Le Pen is the leader of National Front, a far-right political party in France (the pattern continues). She was locked in a tight battle with two other candidates, one who was on the hook for corruption charges and another who is young, ambitious, charismatic and part of the political elite.

In reality this was a race between two: Le Pen and Macron, who leads the incredibly new En Marche! party. Macron formed En Marche! just one year prior to his victory. That's unheard of in the political landscape worldwide.

But it shows that France was desperate for change – change that it didn't really get. Macron is the young charismatic, digitally and technology-focused upstart that has all the charisma of former President Obama and the political savvy of a politician twice his age.

Another way to look at it was that Le Pen was France's "Trump" and Macron is France's "Hillary" (except for the age thing, and charisma thing, and gender thing).

While Le Pen didn't win, the growth and strength of her party was undeniable. Again we see that, while the environment wasn't quite right for these parties now, another bout of the same old, same old might just see the tide finally turn in their favour next time around.

But since then, Macron's policies and leadership have been utter disaster. There has been regular weekly rioting in Paris and other parts of France from the "yellow vest" protests. They've been looting, setting fires, all round social unrest that continues to blight France and the EU.

With Macron failing so badly, perhaps next time around Le Pen wins? And then she too wants France to also leave the EU. She also has made statements regarding the country returning to using their previous currency, the franc.

If German heads into a deep recession, then countries like Italy, Greece and Spain start defaulting on debts, the Eurozone will fall into disarray. Perhaps even disband through sheer incompetence.

Imagine that... or perhaps ask yourself this:

Will the EU be any different in the coming years? Will it continue to favour the establishment? Will it reward the political elite? Will it continue a soft touch approach to immigration and trade? Will it continue to support and bailout greed from European banks and governments addicted to debt?

Will it change at all? And if you think the answer to that question is no, then there's only one way to play the political instability and turmoil of the EU.

***

Very simply, over the next decade we see the EU becoming significantly less powerful. In fact we see other countries following the lead of the UK and exiting the EU. France, Netherlands, Austria, Italy... we think they'll all eventually leave, and the EU will disband.

Brexit alone is going to throw the region into an incredibly difficult period of time. If the EU crumbles and falls apart, countries across the continent will return to managing their own individual affairs. Many will end up returning to their own currencies, like the Netherlands and France want to do.

It will create the most unstable, uncertain and dangerous economic times that Europe has seen since the Second World War – which was the very reason the EU was established to begin with.

With the growing far-right political movements across Europe, currency values could plummet, they would almost certainly become unbearably volatile, and it could create a whole generation of turmoil.

Imagine what that would do to the 743 million people that live in Europe. Imagine the flow-on effect that would have to markets, to currency markets across the entire world!

The situation in Europe now, and the currency devastation that may ensue over the coming years, are so dramatic that people across the world are looking for alternative options to protect their money.

If a situation where multiple countries defaulted on debts and a run on banks were to occur across all of Europe, it could send the world into another global financial crisis. It could lead to the collapse of the global banking system. It would mean payments, transfers, stores of wealth in the traditional banking system (deposits, term deposits, cash) could become worthless and screech to a halt.

The next financial crisis won't be banks failing, but governments.

If the global banking systems then shut down, how will people be able to facilitate any kind of payment?

How will people be able to continue to send money, to buy goods and services, to store wealth in a secure, protected environment where the banks and the government can't get their grubby hands on it while they try and fix the mess they helped create?

There is only one answer, one option to prevent your wealth from disappearing into the ether as the banking system collapses – and that's Bitcoin and cryptocurrency.

There is no doubt in my mind that the EU will fall apart. I see countries going back to old currencies; I see the system becoming harder, more complex and more expensive than ever.

And I see a flight away from the traditional banking system. A flight to an "alternative" banking system. A system that didn't exist during the GFC, but exists today.

While things in Europe are teetering on the edge, there's even more turmoil and currency wars playing out all over the world.

You can also cast your eye over to India, which is going through its own currency crisis. In November 2016 the president went live on TV (unscheduled) to let the country know that in four hours' time – yes just *four hours* – 500 and 1,000 rupee notes would no longer be in circulation and available to citizens – but most importantly, they would not be accepted as legal tender. India *outlawed these bills.*

This stunning move had the intent of trying to eliminate rife corruption, fraud and criminal activity. India has a thriving "black economy". That's also known as the cash economy. And many transactions, many unpaid taxes, many holdings of wealth go unreported – they exist, but never officially in the economy.

The BBC reports that:

> In an attempt to curb tax evasion, the government expects to bring billions of dollars of unaccounted cash into the economy because the banned bills make up more than 80% of the currency in circulation.

> Some 90% of transactions in India are in cash.

This was an astonishing move that – virtually instantly – eroded the cash savings of millions of Indian citizens. Many people across the country held these notes that were now effectively worthless.

This triggered its own state of panic as people crashed the banks to exchange their bills and to withdraw money from their accounts. The fear was that their savings would be further eroded and any semblance of wealth they had would simply disappear.

This had the effect of crashing the rupee. And when you look at the 10-year currency chart of the INR/USD trade, the rupee is at decade-long lows. India set a war on cash, and are going a long way to destroying the wealth of millions of people.

Japan fares no better. There has been a 30-year long period of economic nothingness. They have not seen growth, they have seen a weak currency, and they have lost the dominance they had in the global economy in the 70s and 80s. Japan's economy has simply fallen away to nothing.

China is a tricky one, it clearly understands this could be the whole future of global finance. And rather than sit on its hands, it's actively getting involved in Bitcoin. It sees it as a bridge to get the billions of Chinese connected and into the financial system.

But it has strict controls on who and what can do anything related to the space.

Remember, while China is one of the biggest countries by population in the world, it's still one of the poorest. And China knows this will be a major problem long term.

When you look at (nominal) GDP per capita, China comes in at around US$8,100. The US is around US$57,400. In Australia it's around US$51,800, and in the UK it's at US$40,000.

China has some way to go. But perhaps "decentralised" distributed ledger technology can bring its 1.3 billion into the new crypto financial system, and get it helping to build China's wealth long term.

My view is that China is actively experimenting and involved in this space, but it leaves very little out there for anyone to prove it. I speculate it is building a position in crypto; namely Bitcoin, which could see it emerge as not only just one of the most influential countries in the future success of it, but it may even become one of the biggest holders of it and maybe even use it as a financial instrument like the stores of gold it's reportedly also bulking up on.

Russia is basically in global isolation. It is one of the world's military mighty, but economically is still at the mercy of the US. When it decided to go to war with the Ukraine, the US hit it where it hurts most, economic sanctions.

And let's not forget, in 2015 Russia was in recession. With plummeting oil prices, Russia simply can't balance the books. And it too now realises that it must build a resilient economy, divergent from oil reliance and independent enough from the connections to places like the US or UK to enable long-term economic prosperity.

And where might Russia find this potential decoupling from the traditional economic system? Crypto.

Africa's biggest two problems are the sheer weight of "unbanked" people in the country, and corruption. Imagine if every day African people in all the various countries like Sierra Leone, Uganda, Somalia, Sudan, Libya and Eritrea that weren't caught up in the civil wars and corruption could break free of the shackles of the regimes that dominate those countries.

Imagine if people that have never had access to banking and finance before could use their phones to access a financial system that could help drag them out of poverty. Imagine what could happen if these countries were to suddenly become crypto-friendly and adopt crypto to better the living standards of their people.

While they are some of the most "unbanked" countries in the world, they're also one of the fastest-growing regions for mobile phone and smartphone adoption. If those phones can become part of a global network, a blockchain, then perhaps crypto can pull them up and out into some level of prosperity and future.

And then there's Venezuela!

Venezuela is suffering through a period of hyperinflation and a government again running its country's economy into the ground. The bolivar is becoming increasingly worthless. And it's already seeing a flight to Bitcoin. Venezuelans see Bitcoin as "safer" than the national currency. They are now using Bitcoin to buy goods and services to then smuggle back across the border.

The Venezuelan situation has been one of the most eye-opening use case scenarios for cryptocurrency as a viable alternative in the event of financial collapse we've ever seen.

It's a test case that has outright proven when the system fails, people can rely on crypto to continue to function in commence and economics. It's why the largest spikes in adoption and transactions have been coming from Venezuela which is continuing to fall into disrepair.

Likewise, while not as completely as unstable as Venezuela, Brazil is seeing some of the largest Bitcoin trading volumes ever as more Brazilians look to store some wealth in "digital gold" and protect the value of their money in this alternative financial system.

Hyperinflation makes the cost of something as simple as bread become almost unaffordable overnight. But with restrictions, controls and government interference, people are turning to Bitcoin. They can find some stability in the digital currency, which the government can't stop or control.

As Bitcoin is free from third-party controllers like banks and government, they simply can't touch the Bitcoin and blockchain. It's completely independent of them.

This, of course, has drawn the harsh hand of the Venezuelan government, as it began to shut down local Bitcoin exchanges. But the power of the blockchain can't be stopped, and Bitcoin has now become the "people's money of Venezuela".

This is exactly the situation that makes the whole idea, and ideals of Bitcoin so appealing. It is free. Its freedom puts the power and control of money back in the hands of people and the wider distributed, public network.

It's a big middle finger to government and its inability to

serve the people. In regimes of repression and oppression, Bitcoin shines through. And even in more developed "democracies", Bitcoin has become more than just a digital currency. It's become a movement of freedom from the shackles of the financial elite and a redistribution of power to the people through its decentralised nature.

***

The banking system, the debt addiction, the problems with traditional payments and finance, the political and economic turmoil that's flooding the world – the distrust of government, central banks, FOMO, the rise of decentralised power – you have a seemingly endless stream of perfect conditions that are providing the most incredible environment for something new, revolutionary, transformational to take hold of the world and change the very fabric of society, economies, and the physical world – forever.

Of course, in a time when government and central banks decide on a whim to erode the wealth of citizens, what option do people have to stop it from happening? Well as we know, in the past there was no real way to protect your wealth when a government just decided to take it – that is until people had the ability to shift their wealth out of the traditional banking and finance system, and into an alternative.

And that alternative system is Bitcoin and the blockchain. If there is global financial calamity, there will be a flight to Bitcoin. It will see the value of Bitcoin skyrocket. I envisage that short term the value of just one, single Bitcoin could easily head to US$50,000. And as the turmoil continues and as people realise the benefits of Bitcoin and its future potential, they will flock to it in even greater numbers – pushing the value of just one Bitcoin to well over US$100,000.

If it plays out the way I think – the Europe situation, Brexit, the US's unfathomable spending programmes, US/China trade wars, India's cash war, Venezuela's collapse – it will be the trigger point that starts it all again: another major global financial crisis.

If that's the outcome, then buying up as much Bitcoin as

you can today could become the most important decision you'll ever make in your life.

The crypto economy is going to change everything. And it's so early in its development, so full of potential to revolutionise the world, that for those who can see and seize the opportunity, it's going to mint more "crypto" millionaires and billionaires than the internet. More than the app economy, the tech boom, the oil rush, the Gold Rush, the railroad explosion could ever have imagined.

It starts with Bitcoin and ends with... well, it doesn't end. Bitcoin is the first, the most important, but there is now an ever-expanding universe of crypto that has all the potential of Bitcoin... maybe more to deliver not just potential future wealth, but even perhaps rebuild global networks and infrastructure in a way that restores control and power to where it really belongs, with the people.

And the key events that triggered this revolution show you exactly how the incompetency of central control for the last decade has led to the most transformational change the world has ever seen.

Chapter 7: Events that changed Bitcoin and crypto forever

Before completely getting into the nitty-gritty of how Bitcoin works, how and why you should get some and what its future holds, you should also know about the key moments in its history. This moment-by-moment playbook brings us to where it is today.

Some of the terminology in the list of key events below might be confusing. Or you simply might not know what they mean. But continue on, as I explain them all in Part 2: Genesis.

Then almost like a "choose your own adventure" book, you can revisit these moments and get an even deeper understanding on exactly what it all means and how all the pieces fit together.

That will then bring you to the point we sit at now in 2019 with Bitcoin and the future of the most disruptive financial instrument since the invention of money.

Let's head back to the start...

1. The genesis block

The first ever Bitcoin block as part of the blockchain. This is the "big bang" of Bitcoin. On 3 January 2009 it all started. If you ever get a chance to properly look through the Bitcoin code, you'll see a nice little "Easter egg" buried in it.

There's a piece of data, a reference text that gives weight as to the reason why Bitcoin even exists. Buried in the data there is a piece of text, a reference to the exact day of creation and the global uncertainty that existed in the world at that very moment. The text reads, "The Times 03/Jan/2009 Chancellor on brink of second bailout for banks".

Now if you check the headline of the *Times* newspaper in the UK on that very day of the first genesis block it reads,

"Chancellor on brink of second bailout for banks".

There are two things to learn from this. The first is that, clearly, we know the motivations behind Bitcoin. The second and unproven thing is that perhaps Satoshi Nakamoto is actually British.But if that Easter egg doesn't make you smile a little, then maybe Bitcoin just isn't for you!

2. The first known Bitcoin to USD exchange takes place

Self-proclaimed "Anarchist cyberpunk ninja. A.K.A. Sirius" sold 5,050 BTC for US$5.02 on 12 October 2009. Yes, that equates to just under 1/10th of a cent per Bitcoin. Today that transaction would be roughly worth US$6.26 million. Lots of early users have classic "if only" stories (including me), but surely this one ranks up there... but maybe not as much as the next fella.

3. Bitcoin pizza day

Laszlo Hanyecz becomes the first known user to purchase real goods in exchange for Bitcoin. He goes on to a Bitcoin forum and asks the community on 18 May 2010 if someone will go and buy him two pizzas. In exchange for those pizzas he will transfer (pay) them 10,000 BTC for their troubles.

The US dollar value of 10,000 BTC at the time was about US$25. Making Bitcoin worth around 1/4 of a cent. Hanyecz gets a deal on 22 May and the transaction completes. Hanyecz also becomes infamously known as the million-dollar pizza guy, as those two pizzas (on today's BTC values) would have cost Hanyecz US$27 million. I doubt Hanyecz has ordered a pizza ever since...

But being an online community, every year on 22 May the Bitcoin community celebrates "Bitcoin Pizza Day" in memory of this epic event.

4. Mt. Gox goes live

This is one of the earliest and most well-known Bitcoin

exchanges from the early days of Bitcoin. Based in Tokyo, it launched in July 2010 and at its peak was handling around 70% of all Bitcoin transactions. This was the first exchange I ever used to buy and exchange Bitcoin.

Mt.Gox also had its fair share of troubles, which we'll get to later. But when Mt.- Gox went live and people began to realise this was a unique financial instrument, the price of Bitcoin rose sharply and was then worth 7 US cents.

5. Dollar day

9 February 2011. One Bitcoin is now worth US$1 for the first time since the genesis block. This marks an already incredible rise in price from merely 1/10th of a cent to the magical $1 mark.

People now start to take more notice of Bitcoin in forums, websites and the deep web. Suddenly ecommerce sites start to pop up supporting the use of Bitcoin for payments. In particular on sites in the deep web, Bitcoin is now being used as the "currency" of choice, as it has genuine purchasing power.

6. "The Underground Website Where You Can Buy Any Drug Imaginable"

Adrian Chen publishes his article about Silk Road on the website Gawker on 1 June 2011. It goes viral. All of a sudden major newspapers, news channels and other websites are picking up on this mysterious, unknown and dangerous underworld that exists online.

The whole idea of the dark web, which is really called the deep web amongst technologists, scares the general public. It also gets the attention of the authorities for the first time. It thrusts Bitcoin into the spotlight – making people aware about a digital currency that is anonymous, untraceable and able to be exchanged online for drugs, guns and any illegal thing you can imagine.

While this has negative repercussions to start with, it also supercharges the price of Bitcoin. And on 8 June the price of Bitcoin smashes though US$30 to peak at US$31.60.

However, with its notoriety, the criminal links and with central authorities taking notice, the price plummets *again*. By 12 June the price is now around US$10. This is the kind of volatility that frightens off a lot of the mainstream from taking Bitcoin seriously.

7. Mt.- Gox hack

Eighteen days after Chen's article, Mt.Gox suffers a huge hack. It may be a coincidence that it was hacked after the publication of Chen's article, but that's unlikely. Chen specifically refers to the Mt.- Gox exchange and how it's possible to get some Bitcoins to use on Silk Road.

Opportunistic hackers clearly get wind of some money to be made, and launched themselves at Mt.- Gox's servers. During the hack the nominal price of Bitcoin on the Mt. Gox exchange plummets to just 1 cent as the hackers mess with trades and then withdraw Bitcoin to various accounts. The IP address from the biggest theft came from Hong Kong.

The hacker transfers a large amount to himself, and minutes later user-traded values return to normal prices. Still, it causes Mt.- Gox to come to a grinding halt. At first the company shifts blame on to users as it became clear the stolen amounts had occurred after legitimate user name and login passwords were used to get access to the site.

Until the company realised its database had been stolen and the hackers were logging in with *real user names and passwords* from a stolen database. Mt.- Gox had to roll back all the fraudulent sell orders and restore the market to around US$17.50 per BTC.

8. Bitcoin goes primetime

Bitcoin gets its Hollywood moment on an episode of the US TV Show *The Good Wife* called *Bitcoin for Dummies*. According to the episode guide:

> *Alicia's client is being pressured to reveal the name of the anonymous Bitcoin creator so that the government can prosecute him for creating what they believe to be*

a currency in direct competition with the US dollar.

While this was massive attention for Bitcoin, by this stage Bitcoin had mainly fallen from the mainstream media and there is still little public knowledge or awareness still of what it really is.

Most people I spoke to around this time really don't know about it, how it works, other than it's some kind of "internet money". And when *The Good Wife* episode airs, the price of Bitcoin is languishing at around US$5. The incredible volatility terrifies most people, and the debate about the longevity and relevance of Bitcoin intensifies among the online technology community.

9. 2012, hack-city

While the Mt. Gox hack in 2011 was major, it's nothing compared to what comes during 2012. Firstly in March, Linode is hacked. Linode is a cloud server company that hosted Bitcoin-trading platforms. Online web news portal Ars Technica confirms that 46,703 BTC are stolen in the hack, which were worth around US$228,845 at the time.

By August, Bitcoin Savings and Trust, a company enticing investors with 7% weekly return on investment, and its lead manager, Trendon T. Shavers, manages to defraud Bitcoin users out of somewhere between 82,000 and 500,000 BTC – no one really knows the exact amount.

The US Securities and Exchange Commission (SEC) would eventually press charges and convict Shavers in 2013 for operating a Ponzi scheme to defraud investors. But with the SEC getting involved in a Bitcoin-related case, the questions again start to come to the surface about how regulators and governments should treat Bitcoin.

Is it a currency, an asset, property...? How do they tax it? No one really knows, and there's no one universal solution. The borderless nature of Bitcoin makes it virtually impossible for regulators to manage, and that makes it an enemy of the state.

10. You get... half

At the end of 2012, on 28 November, one of the most significant events in Bitcoin history takes place – the block reward for mining halves.

Instead of a 50 BTC reward for mining a block, miners now get just 25 BTC. This changes the economics of Bitcoin mining *significantly*. All of a sudden the hobbyists at home with a PC and a couple of graphic processing units (GPUs) start to get pushed out of the mining market with more ferocity. Adding to this is the rise in application specific integrated circuit (ASIC) miners, which are dedicated mining rigs. Furthermore, these ASICs are being bundled together to create ASIC mining pools – basically supercomputers just for mining Bitcoin.

In other words, entire companies are now popping up around the world whose sole aim is to mine Bitcoin for profit. The biggest surge in dedicated miners and mining companies occurs in China. Around this time on 31 December 2012, Bitcoin is again heading north and is trading at US$13.51.

11. 2013 – Greece, the US, Cyprus

We won't delve into this too much more (see earlier chapter). While these major countries' debt and default concerns plague global markets, a lot of other events are taking place in the Bitcoin community.

These other events, combined with the global turmoil, create the perfect storm that will see one BTC hit more than US$1,150 by the end of November 2013.

12. Coinbase tops $1 million

In February 2013 Coinbase, a company built around the processing of Bitcoin payments for merchants wanting to accept Bitcoin, says it has sold more than US$1 million in Bitcoin in a single month, with an average price over US$22 per BTC.

13. The banking crisis in Cyprus

This crisis sends Bitcoin skyrocketing. Thanks to a run on Cypriot banks in March, by 1 April 2013 Bitcoin pushes through *US$100* for the first time ever.

Nine days later it peaks at US$263.48. Two days after that on 12 April the price crashes hard to just US$67.60. After the insane volatility in 2011 and 2012, this only reaffirms the fear people have of buying and holding Bitcoin as any kind of investment.

Most people simply can't stomach seeing the fiat value of their Bitcoin go up and down so rapidly.

14. Law enforcement gets involved

On 23 June 2013 the US Drug Enforcement Agency lists 11.02 BTC as a seized asset belonging to Eric Daniel Hughes. This is assumed to be the first ever instance of a law enforcement agency seizing actual Bitcoins from an individual.

It's also believed that this seizure is in relation to a sting involving Silk Road. But from the end of April through to the end of September, there is not much going on in the world of Bitcoin. And then...

15. The king is dead

If you went into the deep web and found your way through to Silk Road on Wednesday 2 October 2013 you will not have found what you were looking for. Instead you will have seen two large symbols, one belonging to the US Department of Justice, and another belonging to the US Federal Bureau of Investigation (FBI).

And you will have seen in large, bold text, "This Hidden Site Has Been Seized". At the beginning of October the FBI managed to find the mysterious and elusive alleged owner of Silk Road, a user by the name of Dread Pirate Roberts – or as the FBI believed it to be, Ross William Ulbricht.

This wasn't some well-organised bust on a suburban house where the feds kicked down doors and threw in smoke grenades. No, Ulbricht was arrested at the *San Francisco Public Library*.

The FBI charges against Ulbricht said Silk Road was "the most sophisticated and extensive criminal marketplace on the Internet today." The FBI also alleges that he has around 600,000 Bitcoins – worth at the time around US$80 million (today worth around US$1.6 billion).

The FBI shuts down Silk Road and prosecutes Ulbricht. Today he is currently serving a life sentence without possibility of parole. The Ulbricht arrest and Silk Road closure sends the price of Bitcoin from US$125.31 to US$84.07 *in just three hours!* By midnight 4 October, the price of Bitcoin bounces strongly back to US$121.29. This shows how volatile but also how resilient this crypto asset is now becoming.

16. The US Senate wants a say

18 November, 2013 the US Senate holds a hearing on Bitcoin, "Beyond Silk Road: Potential Risks, Threats, and Promises of Virtual Currencies". Ulbricht's arrest has put the cryptocurrency front and square with the US authorities and regulators.

They want to figure out how to handle this "digital currency". Surprisingly they affirm that they don't want to stand in the way of innovation. But clearly they want to protect the interests of the US dollar, taxation and how people operate in the existing banking system. The links of Bitcoin to criminal enterprise put it in the line of sight of authorities.

17. Even China weighs in

20 November, the price of Bitcoin is now trading upwards around US$645 per BTC. The hype is continuing to build. People are meeting in cafes to exchange Bitcoin through their smartphones. There's even a Bitcoin ATM in downtown Vancouver.

Then the People's Bank of China weighs in on the Bitcoin debate. And it decides to give it the green light. It declares "that people should be free to participate in the Bitcoin market". For such a tightly-controlled regime to open the floodgates to such a disruptive financial and economic instrument sends the price ballistic.

18. US$1,000 and beyond

The culmination of the US debt ceiling, fears of another banking crisis, trouble in Europe, bailouts, bail-ins and threat of all-out financial Armageddon strike again. This, added to China and the US laying a favourable eye to people's involvement in Bitcoin, and things go nuts.

Bitcoin turns up and heads north with such ferocity that every major news outlet in the world once again begins to cover Bitcoin. The speed and veracity of its price movements make it akin to "Tulip mania" in Renaissance Holland. On 28 November 2013 one Bitcoin becomes worth more than US$1,000. Two days later on 30 November the price of Bitcoin peaks at US$1,156.

19. China says yes, China says NO!

In an astonishing about-turn on 5 December, China decides that it's now going to impose restrictions on Bitcoin. It declares that it's not a currency and prohibits all financial institutions in China from dealing with, exchanging, trading or offering any kind of services related to Bitcoin.

At this point Bitcoin has been highly volatile and trading around US$1,000 for about a few days. After the Chinese announcement it plummets to US$909. By 18 December the price of Bitcoin is now back to US$522.

20. Mt. Gox disappears

After Mt. Gox rose to such dominance as an early market platform for Bitcoin, it came to a just as an abrupt halt. On 14 February 2014 Mt. Gox simply vanished. Users couldn't log into the site, there was nothing anyone could do.

People with Bitcoin sitting in online wallets within the Mt. Gox system simply couldn't access their account to even move their Bitcoin out of the Mt. Gox system. Mt. Gox went bankrupt, and the company lost over 744,000 BTC.

I had a nominal amount of Bitcoin in a Mt. Gox wallet that had been sitting in there for a year or two, but it just vanished – along with others who probably held far more than I did. Eventually, CEO Mark Karpeles would be arrested and charged in Japan. He was released from prison on bail in July 2016, but must remain in Japan – on "Japan arrest".

21. The US gets it all so wrong

The US government had been trying to figure out exactly what to do about Bitcoin for over two years by 2014. Eventually in March 2014 the Internal Revenue Service decided that Bitcoin is not a currency, but instead is "property". The idea was that it could treat it in the same way it treats stocks and barter transactions.

Needless to say, this decision baffles many, and goes against the fundamental purpose of Bitcoin. For example, if you buy a $5 sandwich using Bitcoin and those Bitcoin's cost you $2, you would have to pay capital gains tax on the $3 differential. Make sense? Of course it doesn't. This proves central authorities simply have no idea about Bitcoin.

But this decision sent the price of Bitcoin from US$586 plummeting down to US$360 by 10 April 2014 as people in the US are bamboozled by the government's interference.

22. Dell and Microsoft think maybe this is OK

The real potential of Bitcoin starts to bubble to the surface during 2014. This is emphasised by more and more merchants accepting Bitcoin as payment for goods and services. In particular, computing giant Dell, which decides it will accept Bitcoin as payment. Dell uses Coinbase as its Bitcoin payments processor.

Then in December 2014 the biggest of all merchant announcements comes through... Microsoft says it will accept Bitcoin as payment for apps, games and content online through Windows and Xbox online.

23. Size matters

Perhaps the biggest ongoing debate around the inner

circles of Bitcoin development is the size of Bitcoin blocks. As the blockchain system gets larger and larger, more transactions need processing every day. The current block size is 1MB. And there is a division amongst developers over whether it should be 2MB, or even larger.

This kicks off in 2015 when Bitcoin XT – a hard fork from the Bitcoin client system – goes live. This fork (an alternative version of the same thing that runs parallel to the original) has the Bitcoin community divided. If the blocks stay at 1MB, it lends itself to a natural market for transaction fees. But the system simply won't be able to scale globally while maintaining speed and ease.

If the block is larger it will speed up transactions but make the fees less, which doesn't incentivise miners (nodes) as much as higher transaction fees would. But more users mean more transactions and ultimately more fees.

In short, to scale Bitcoin to billions of people and billions of transactions per day it must get faster. Otherwise it ends up more like a digital version of physical gold. When this debate started back in 2015 (and it's still going) it sent the market into a panic about disagreement and dissent among Bitcoin's core developers.

It was during this initial turmoil within the community that Bitcoin traded at its lowest since right before the hype and peak in 2013. Two years later in 2015, Bitcoin had gone through the kind of volatility that no financial instruments has ever seen, survived, and come out stronger at the other end.

The end of 2015 and start of 2016 would see stability begin to creep into Bitcoin, even with the "scaling debate" never really going away. Soon wiser heads and more unemotional views surface with the idea that perhaps this really could become an alternative, global payments system. And the driving idea is that the blockchain technology that Bitcoin is founded upon could be the most influential technology of the 21st century.

24. The trust machine

The potential of the blockchain as a disruptive financial

technology is highlighted when The *Economist* publishes a front-page article on Bitcoin titled "The Trust Machine" in October 2015. It explains how, "The technology behind Bitcoin could transform how the economy works." It goes on to point out Bitcoin has an unfairly shady image due to its early ties to the deep web and Silk Road.

It also highlights the fact that, when you really look at the technology and how Bitcoin works, there is tremendous potential to revolutionise how the world's economies and payment systems operate in an increasingly digital and interconnected world.

25. OpenBazaar

The ultimate, legal and community-minded marketplace goes live – OpenBazaar. This is a peer-to-peer (P2P) program that users download, which connects directly to other people who are looking to buy or sell goods and services. This is like an open-source, community-focused eBay, Amazon and Gumtree all rolled into one huge P2P platform.

The *only accepted currency* on OpenBazaar is Bitcoin. This is the beginning of widespread ecommerce adoption outside of major corporations. Venture capital heavyweights Union Square Ventures and Andreessen Horowitz invested US$1 million to help fund OpenBazaar's development. At the time of launch Bitcoin was worth US$420.

26. You got half, now you now get half of that

It happened on 28 November 2012. And on 9 July 2016 it happened again. The reward for mining a block of Bitcoin halves again. At the beginning the reward was 50 Bitcoin. Then it halves to 25. From 9 July it is now 12.5 Bitcoin per block.

As more blocks are mined, the reward will continue to halve around every 250,000 blocks. Eventually, predicted to be sometime around the year 2140, all Bitcoin will be mined and there will be no more Bitcoin rewards. Mining will cease. Miners will instead turn into transaction processors and be rewarded with transaction fees.

27. Trump. Europe. Brexit.

Reminiscent of 2013, the world re-enters familiar territory. Except this time it's government around the world forming from right-wing, interventionist and introspective policy. Trade wars and currency wars seem to be bubbling up to the surface. Politically, the world is in turmoil – and Bitcoin's fiat conversion price is benefiting. In 2016 and into 2017, with so much global instability, the price of Bitcoin again marches onwards and upwards past US$1,000.

28. The cryptocurrency boom

Bitcoin is not alone. The truth is Bitcoin hasn't been on its own since the start. But in terms of mainstream awareness it wasn't until 2017 that the world stood up and took notice of not just Bitcoin but all cryptocurrencies.

Incredible growth in other "crypto" such as Ethereum, Ripple, NEM, PivX, Dash and others saw early investors from the 2013/14 days see their investments increase 1,000%, 5,000% 10,000% and more in the space of just a few months. Many call it the "cryptocurrency bubble", but the truth is the world is only just starting to wake up to the fact that cryptocurrency (not just Bitcoin) is building a whole new financial system, a new social architecture. The most significant and powerful technological revolution in the history of mankind. The crypto revolution started in 2013, but it only really began in 2017.

The 2017 boom catches the attention of the mainstream, but it's another boom that really gets speculators running wild.

29. ICO Mania

The ICO isn't a new concept to crypto. As far back as 2013 new cryptocurrencies would launch to market. Some of the early ones just distributed the crypto to users in the community. Soon enough it was realised this was a good way to fund a project from concept to release. And crypto started selling tokens in ICOs to launch new projects. This coincided with the exponential rise in value of Bitcoin.

As Bitcoin headed north through $1,000, $4,000, $8,000, $10,000, $15,000 and right up to US$20,000, crypto projects with nothing more than a PowerPoint presentation, nice website and a good idea were raising millions of dollars in crypto in ICOs. Some were selling out in seconds. Filecoin, one of the biggest, raised over US$257 million in September 2017 in a month-long ICO. EOS ran a year-long ICO that brought in an astounding... wait for it... US$4 billion.

The ICO boom was like nothing else crypto had ever seen. Tokens were gaining 10, 20 times their ICO price when listing on exchanges. Extreme FOMO had kicked in once more and were delivering real gains to money that was getting in and out fast.

30. Civil war

Bitcoin's scaling debate comes to a head and two competing factions within the developer and miner communities surface. The debate is how to best implement scale for Bitcoin. There's no doubt that now, with more users, the network is slowing.

Scaling isn't something that just "should" be done. It must be done. Thankfully, in June 2017 there seems to be consensus as over 80% of the network agree to SegWit, a scaling proposal that at least short term will speed up the network. This is necessary to at the very least improve speed and security in Bitcoin, and shows that even though the threat of civil war can bubble to the surface, ultimately the community will come to a consensus. It's in the interests of all to keep Bitcoin going and moving forward.

This is the first sign that trouble internally can be overcome by the network. It's proof that decentralised organisation can organise, mobilise and operate outside of centralised control. This is a significant moment, and proof that, long term Bitcoin is heading on the right track for widespread, global adoption.

31. Forked off

Civil war ended, but not as expected. Instead of a universal consensus, the competing communities just decided to split and go their separate ways. This resulted in Bitcoin's hard fork and the creation of Bitcoin Cash.

One decided they knew how to implement change for the betterment of Bitcoin, the other decided a different way was needed. There's still civil war as each hates the other and they compete with great toxicity towards each other.

But that's not the end of it. When you thought one fork was enough, a whole range of projects saw easy money up for grabs and decided to fork from Bitcoin's main code and create their own version of how Bitcoin should succeed. There's now things like Bitcoin Dark, Bitcoin Private, Super Bitcoin, Bitcoin Gold and Bitcoin SV.

Each claims to be the real Bitcoin. But none of them, I repeat, none of them, are even close to the strength and dominance of the original Bitcoin chain. Bitcoin Cash is the closest, but even it is nowhere near the significance of the original Bitcoin, and there's a good chance none of them will ever get to the same level.

32. The peak

When I first published this book, it was before the parabolic rise in crypto towards the end of 2017 and start of 2018. Here's what I predicted the short-term nature of Bitcoin would end up like...

> In 2018 Bitcoin will breach through the US$10,000 barrier. This milestone was thought to be impossible. But with activated developments to the blockchain and the scaling debate now well past, Bitcoin will be able to grow, scale and bring in more users around the world.
>
> The global "unbanked" will begin to adopt it and use it to involve themselves in finance and wealth creation. Merchants will come on board, accepting it as payment. Innovative companies will find ways to allow Bitcoin to be accepted as a payment method, just like cash.
>
> The exponential growth of the network will continue to push the price of one Bitcoin higher. And early

investors will begin to see the kind of growth and return on investment – and ability to use their Bitcoin in the real world – that they can financially operate outside of the "traditional" banking system.

Well, I was kind of right. Except Bitcoin sailed through US$10,000 and marched as high as US$20,000 at its peak in early 2018. This was the utter height of crypto FOMO.

Daily crypto reports were appearing on news channels like CNN and MSNBC, Fox Business and Bloomberg. There was an explosion of financial experts that wanted their two cents on crypto in the mainstream media, they were on the balance of things horribly wrong and helped fuel FOMO that was about to implode.

From this peak we would see the collapse of crypto prices. We would see the destruction of the ICO market. And in 2018 and 2019 the "crypto winter" would grip the crypto markets.

33. Crypto winter

At the peak of FOMO and hysteria in early 2018 it seemed as though everyone and anyone was a "guru" of crypto investing. I remember being at a wedding and word got out I was involved in crypto. Soon after, at least a half dozen men, all in their 30s, started hitting me about crypto.

The scary part was that they all seemed to have a different crypto they were trying to shill (shill means to pump and promote) to each other. None of these guys had been involved in crypto more than a few months, but all were experts... apparently.

Interestingly, it seemed this peak was particularly attractive to speculative, punters, mainly men, mainly appealing to "bro culture".

Sadly many of them would get burnt as crypto values dive-bombed. And it wasn't just the ICO market that the arse end fell out of. All major crypto across the board headed south. And by the end of 2018 even Bitcoin was trading down around the US$3,200 mark.

The bubble had burst... or you'd think that was the case. This prolonged downtrend and collapse in fiat-converted prices was devastating to many who bought in chasing gains at the top.

But this wasn't a bubble collapsing, it was a part of the short and ferocious crypto cycle. This was a pattern we'd seen repeat in Bitcoin twice before and in altcoins (alternative coins) once earlier in 2013.

This period widely became known as the "crypto winter". A period where it seemed that nothing was even going to be like it was again during the golden times of late 2017 and 2018.

But as I say, this is a phenomenon that for those of us who've been around crypto long enough will know is a part of crypto investing. And it's a cycle that's got every chance of repeating again in the future.

But what these periods of "winter" really do is help to consolidate the space. You find the junk gets wiped clear and the quality projects and crypto that have real use case potential and longevity knuckle down and get on with the job.

Crypto winter is akin to the ashes that the tech bubble left behind in 2000. Yes it was devastating at the time, but the quality remained and continued to build and develop. And from that some of the world's most influential organisations rose.

Well, that's what this most recent crypto winter is doing. The ones that have been able to survive have continued to thrive. In fact this has been an opportunity to progress the development of crypto further than most people can appreciate.

And while in fiat-converted prices it might seem like a crypto winter, the truth is the crypto ecosystem during this period has never been stronger, and more advanced.

34. Buidl

In crypto there's a phrase used to describe holding strong on to tokens for future gain. The term is "hodl".

Its origins are a spelling mistake from a semi-drunk forum post on Bitcointalk. The writer meant to say "hold" but the spelling mistake was an easy one to make, and due to the niche nature of crypto communities back then, it kind of stuck around.

But more recently the term, "buidl" has come to the fore. It's a play on the term hodl, but buidl is supposed to signify the idea of "build".

That means the community continuing to develop and advance projects and achieve their stated goals. It also means the innovation of existing blockchains, crypto and the launch of new game-changing opportunities.

Over the last few years the idea of buidl has continued to gain momentum, particularly during the crypto winter. It is the community showing progress in the seeming face of adversity.

However when you live and breathe crypto day in, day out and are involved with the inner workings of it all, you can see that the strength of the buidl movement has never been more important.

While the world around continues to dive into turmoil, fear and uncertainty, the construction of crypto infrastructure, and innovation of existing networks proves that this isn't a fly-by-night fad. More importantly, it's a rebuilding of the world's connective networks.

Buidl is now as significant and important as hodl, the two together combine to create a force for global change, the likes of which we've never seen.

35. The future...

The truth is, no one really knows how big crypto could really end up. How widespread and widely accepted it could become is a matter of conjecture at such an early stage of its development.

My view is that by 2027 Bitcoin will become the world's global reserve currency. You will be able to get paid in Bitcoin. You will be able to spend your Bitcoin in Australia, the UK, the US, Europe, anywhere in the world as it becomes the first real borderless global currency.

It will be a truly global alternative financial system outside of the influence and control of central authorities like central banks, governments and major financial institutions.

With this kind of widespread adoption, people will talk about the price of goods and services in "Satoshi" – part Bitcoin – not in whole Bitcoin any more. People will be able to buy daily goods and services, groceries, energy, consumer goods, cars... houses with their Satoshi.

And those that hold whole Bitcoin will have their wealth multiplied times over as the price of Bitcoin exceeds the fiat equivalent of US$100,000 and pushes on to US$1,000,000. Of course comparison to fiat currency is moot by this point, because there's no real need to use country specific currency. Bitcoin will be so widely accepted that you'll be able to use it anywhere, anytime to operate in the global crypto economy.

Supply chains will use Bitcoin so pricing will shift from fiat denominations to crypto denomination, with Bitcoin as the main base pair. In short, the future is a continuance of the crypto revolution, and with more milestones and major developments to come, I expect this current list of 34 major events that have shaped Bitcoin and crypto so far, will expand to a very, very large list.

Now with Part One under your belt, the next big topics to tackle are what exactly is Bitcoin – technically speaking. How do you get it, store it, spend it, sell it and operate in the crypto economy?

PART TWO:
Genesis

Part One is designed to give you a reference point when you start to consider why Bitcoin and crypto hold such significant value and massive potential. It helps you to understand the backstory as to why it even exists to start with.

In Part Two I'm going to dig a little deeper into the more intricate details of Bitcoin to start with, including what it *really* is and how it works from a technical perspective (I'll make it as easy and simple for you to understand as possible).

I'll also outline how you can go about getting it, buying it, using it and storing it. And yes, that's right, I absolutely believe you should be buying and storing Bitcoin – I'll explain why in Part Two, also.

And then I'll expand your horizons and introduce you to a list of other crypto that we believe holds all the kind of potential that Bitcoin had in its early days. These crypto could be looking at a wealth-creation opportunity the same size if not bigger than Bitcoin – they should be on your radar and should encourage you to take your research and understanding of crypto markets that little bit further beyond my book.

But first, to understand Bitcoin and the wider crypto markets and their potential and other non-Bitcoin crypto, you need to understand how the global payments and monetary system works today. This can get complex, and I'll try to keep it as simple as I can. But, inherently, the global banking system is complex, hard to understand and difficult to use, which is exactly what makes Bitcoin so full of potential for the world in the coming years.

So let's dive in...

Chapter 8: Gold? Stocks? Cash? Property? What is Bitcoin?

The name Bitcoin itself does no favours to people trying to understand exactly what it is. Upon first glance people naturally assume it's a "coin", a currency that you use.

And in some aspects of Bitcoin's intent and origins, yes it is indeed a currency. But it's more than that. Bitcoin is like nothing else the world has ever seen before. And as such, we shouldn't try and compare it to gold, stocks, cash, currency – it's unique in so many ways. That's what I'll explain to you here.

A good place to start with what exactly Bitcoin is, is to simply think about it as nothing. Drop any preconceived idea that it's like gold, stocks, cash or whatever.

Think about it at its base level as simply some lines of computer code. Code with extremely tight cryptography principles and mathematics, which make it like no other financial instrument before.

That doesn't make it hard to use. It actually makes it secure when you consider how you then get Bitcoin and how its "blockchain" functions, but more on that later.

Another good place to start with, to understand why it's so radically different to anything we've seen before, is to understand the basic concepts of currency that we use today.

***

Barter was a system of exchange people used thousands of years ago.

The basic premise is:

I have an asset that you want, you have an asset I want, and we exchange said assets in a way we both deem to be fair.

For example, you might have a chicken that lays eggs and I want eggs. Conversely, I have a cow and you want milk.

We come to an arrangement whereby you give me a dozen eggs and I give you four pints of milk.

Simple. But basic. And in that sense your eggs have "currency" to me and my milk has "currency" to you.

Now as simple as this is, it works. But when it comes to the exchange of other goods, or the bartering of assets where the two parties can't decide on a fair trade, the system basically falls down.

Bartering was always a system that would fall away in a more complex world of commerce. And in its place came money.

Now, when you really think about it, money is simply a device that allows ubiquitous trade amongst people who share and hold different resources. It is by nature a belief system. If I put faith in that currency as worth something, and we all have that same fundamental belief system in place, then it's worth something.

That allows more complex transactions. I might have 20 cows, you 20 chickens and Bob across the road 20 pigs. You want a cow, I want a pig and Bob wants a chicken.

I'm not giving you a cow for your chicken because I don't want it.

And Bob isn't giving me a pig for a cow, as he wants your chicken.

So instead our government decides to issue money. So we exchange this money for those goods. In return for helping us to facilitate our commerce, the government take a clip from us in taxes, penalties or some other means.

How much money I have to give anyone is dependent on the market value for each of the cow, chicken or pig. I give Bob four coins for his pig. That's the price we deem fair. He now has three coins that he can give to you for your chicken – but perhaps the agreed worth of the chicken is only two coins. But Bob decides to get two chickens. Now you have four coins. And as you want my cow and a cow is worth four coins (like a pig), you give me four coins for my cow.

It's a complex transaction made super simple. But that's how money flows around the economy. People buy things, sell things, goods, services, skills – in exchange for money, which they go on to use in other parts of an economy.

Let's stop there for a second.

You see, in the physical world, at its core we have been using money/cash for hundreds of years to operate commerce. We work, earn money and then spend it or save it. We spend it to purchase things we need and things we want. We save it to purchase things we need and things we want later in the future.

This cycle of money in and out of our hands is what drives economies and corporations. It's also what funds governments as they tax us, fine us, and take money from us to operate and exercise their will and control.

Now all this money was grand. Until some people decided they wanted something but didn't have enough money for it. So along the way the world also developed this thing called debt. Debt is an "IOU" to someone to pay them money at a later date. I might want a pig and two chickens but have just four coins. So I go to another person with four coins and say, "If you give me your four coins, I'll give you five coins next week." Then I have eight coins to get the pig and two chickens. But I now also have to figure out how to get those four coins and one extra back to that person by next week.

If I don't, they have a right to take my pig (which is worth more than one coin!) because that's the deal we struck.

In modern times most people understand debt because the biggest amount they'll ever take on is to buy a house.

The reason someone uses debt is because they don't have enough money now to buy what they want or need. So they use debt with the view to pay the money to the person (or institution) lending it to them at a later date.

The global financial system we live in has, over time, made it easier and easier to get debt. So much so that, often, debt is used to fund debt. And as more debt is issued the value of your money actually erodes. This is particularly evident when governments take on debt.

Now, I could write a whole separate book solely about the banking and financial system, debt and the mismanagement of economies.

I could write far more about how twisted and deceptive governments are. Books about how the entire financial system is fuelled with debt and how currency wars are building to the crescendo of another giant almighty financial catastrophe... or not.

And I touched on currency wars, political turmoil, the financial system, debt and its root in the origins of Bitcoin, in Part One. But the trail of destruction that it's all left behind will never be forgotten.

That's fundamentally why, instead of the money that we use to circulate within the borders of our home countries, we now have another option.

With all the debt built up in the world, and central banks printing more money to fund and fuel this debt, they are eroding the wealth of everyday citizens like yourself. What started as a basic concept to enable commerce around the world, developed into this all-consuming beast we know as the global financial system. It's far too complex, convoluted and corrupt. It's a broken system that needs an alternative... and that alternative is now here.

Think about it like this. Are you sick of governments ripping you off? Are you sick of banks and giant multinational corporations ripping you off? Of the political elites and establishment ripping you off?

Are you sick of this debt addiction from governments that your great grandkids will be left to pay for?

If you are worried, then the answer is Bitcoin.

Bitcoin in its purest description – from the Satoshi Nakamoto white paper – is, "A purely peer-to-peer version of electronic cash". It allows the transfer of payments from one party to another without going through a financial institution.

It cuts out intermediaries and middlemen. It allows people to buy pigs and chickens and cows without a central issuing and controlling authority.

Its aim is to reduce barriers, cost and borders of global finance. It was and is for *everyone*, to benefit *everyone*. Not just the elite, not just the powerful and already wealthy. It's the libertarian, anti-establishment, alternative digital financial system.

And (at least to begin with) Bitcoin was also built around anonymity.

It achieves a level of anonymity because its core code is based around cryptography, mathematics and encryption. That's also worth noting. At the end of the day, Bitcoin, or any cryptocurrency for that matter, is nothing more than computer code – at least literally.

And to many people the idea that something so intangible can have tangible value is a difficult concept to overcome. But once they do, and once they become a part of the belief system that says Bitcoin *is* worth something and *can* be used as a medium of exchange for goods and services, then it's inherently worth something. This is regardless of there being no physical "good" to back it. And besides the money you now use, that's really only backed by debt – that's even more intangible than Bitcoin's code.

Remember, Bitcoin is unique in that nothing like it has existed before with the capacity for widespread mass adoption and mass belief.

Continuing on with the privacy aspect. The way in which Bitcoin attains its quasi-anonymity is via the use of what is known as "private keys" (a form of encryption). In that way, only the holder of a private key can have access to the corresponding wallet that the private key opens.

Each wallet also has a "public key", which is the address that users use to make transactions. But privacy can be maintained as the public keys are unidentifiable to a particular user. And as long as private keys are kept private, then no third party can access a wallet.

By using this method of public and private keys, third

parties and counterparties can be removed from the flow of payments from one to another. It means that a user becomes their own bank, responsible for the storage, safety and transactions to and from their wallets.

This enable peers (you and I and anyone else) on the network to send payments and make transactions. We can do this with safety and security as the network that records the transactions "signs" these transactions using public keys to verify the transfer from one "wallet" to another. And this process of signing and confirming transactions within the network means that the network is 100% accurate and foolproof.

The network itself becomes the trusted source – but as the network is distributed amongst the users, everyone is a part of the in-built trust of the network.

In short, with Bitcoin you simply make transactions through its network, which is known as a "blockchain". In making transactions through the blockchain from one location to another, no bank, no government, no third party or intermediaries touches it, sees it or has anything to do with it. It is completely peer-to-peer, and it is (mostly) anonymous.

The anonymity of Bitcoin was part of its initial appeal. But this aspect also drew the ire of authorities and lawmakers. This was particularly controversial as Bitcoin was the primary payment method through the deep web and on illegal goods sites like Silk Road. And sure, to this day it's still a form of payment for illegal activity because of this – but so is physical cash.

While the use of public and private keys with Bitcoin allowed the senders and receivers to remain anonymous (and still does), all transactions on the blockchain are still a matter of public record.

For example, I can send you 1 Bitcoin from my Bitcoin wallet. All I need is your public key. All you ever see is my public key. We can't access each other's wallets because neither of us has access to the other's private key. All we see is the anonymous public key.

Now, if I don't know you, then I can't identify you through

your wallet address. And vice versa.

However, you and I and the blockchain might not know who we're dealing with, but the whole blockchain sees that transaction of 1 Bitcoin. It sees how much data is used to make that transaction, it sees the amount of confirmations – it gets enough info in the transaction that it can be verified and even traced back to a particular location or IP address, using some very laborious tracking techniques.

And this is ultimately where Bitcoin has been proved to be almost anonymous – but not 100%.

By monitoring the data transfer from one wallet to another, eventually you can actually identify a wallet and assign it to a particular user. Of course, this is an extremely laborious task for a casual user to achieve. It requires being able to monitor data flow from wallets and from IP addresses at any given moment. Pretty complex stuff.

So for most people, using Bitcoin is still anonymous. But if the National Security Agency (NSA), Government Communications Headquarters (GCHQ) or Australian Signals Directorate (ASD) wanted to track your Bitcoin movements, then they have the resources to likely be able to confidently identify you. Still, as long as you're not doing anything illegal to begin with, then it's unlikely you'll ever appear on the radar of such agencies.

So remember, it's mostly anonymous and private – but if you're a nasty character, or on a wanted list somewhere, watch out!

Of course, when it comes to Bitcoin's anonymity, its core purpose, the ability to exist as a medium of exchange and a store of value and how it can even exist, we do still need to head back to that very beginning – to the genesis block of Bitcoin...

***

In the years since publishing the Bitcoin white paper, the real identity of Satoshi Nakamoto has never been revealed.

There have been claims to be the Satoshi Nakamoto, most notably a man from Sydney, Australia, named Craig Wright. But there has never been any concrete evidence this is the case.

Nonetheless, Wright is still trying to pursue hundreds of Bitcoin-related patents in what appears to be an "intellectual property land grab", according to Reuters.

Maybe Wright is, maybe he's not, now it's somewhat irrelevant and the ideal of "Satoshi" is almost as important a part of the mysterious allure of Bitcoin as the idea of cryptocurrency itself.

Perhaps we'll never find out who the original Satoshi Nakamoto is. Maybe they're hiding in plain sight. Maybe we don't need to know – or should know. The idea is now bigger than the creator, and that is perhaps the best way for it to stay.

In my view, it's probably best that we never find out, as the mystery adds to the ideal of what Bitcoin could end up becoming.

To help get your head around Bitcoin, one of the best pieces of advice I can give is to read the actual Bitcoin white paper by Nakamoto. It's not very long, and it's reasonably simple. In reading the complete white paper, it's also important to understand the timing of the release.

Remember, as I explained in Part One, the whole timing of the Bitcoin white paper came off the back of the global financial crisis and a world addicted to debt, suffering from political instability and turmoil – a world at war, financial war.

When you read the white paper, you'll understand that it is fundamentally anti-financial system, anti-establishment and anti-corporate greed.

It provides an alternative financial system to the one we currently use to buy things, sell things, transfer money around the world and build our "traditional" financial wealth.

As I said, the white paper by Nakamoto is a *must-read*. I

implore you to read it after you've finished with this book, and before you go and get some Bitcoin for yourself.

In time, the release of the Bitcoin white paper will go down as one of the most important global events of all time. It will surpass the significance of any treaty, agreement, law or constitution that exists. It will sit alongside the Magna Carta when people think of significant historical documents.

I also compare reading the Nakamoto white paper to reading Alan Turing's paper on the Imitation Game. It too is something worth reading if just for its vision of how artificial intelligence (AI) will develop.

Admittedly, the Imitation Game is longer and a little more complex. But both are proving to be incredibly important to our high-tech future.

And what Turing's Imitation Game is to computing and AI, Nakamoto's paper is to global finance.

But should you not feel like taking the time to read Nakamoto's white paper, let us boil things down to one simple question: what is Bitcoin?

The white paper outlines it in a nutshell, Bitcoin is a digital currency.

Nakamoto explains this in the white paper. He writes that it is an electronic coin, by definition, which is just a "chain of digital signatures".

And like a currency that exists in fiat money (USD, AUD, GBP) you can get it, spend it, save it, give it away or even steal it (if you're criminally inclined). The reality is that Bitcoin's design is to be much like any other fiat currency, but for one key difference: There is no central control, and it remains predominately anonymous.

Let's go back again to the earlier example with cows, pigs and chickens. You can simply replace "money" with "Bitcoin". If you want cows or chickens or pigs, the future will enable you to pay for those goods with Bitcoin.

The difficulty that currently exists with Bitcoin as a

"currency", however, is its comparative fiat value. For example, let's say the price of one Bitcoin is US$10,000 and I want to buy a US$3 coffee.

Now the smallest denomination of Bitcoin is 0.00000001 BTC. That's also known as 1 Satoshi. So if I want that coffee, then I've got to pay the coffee shop 0.0003 BTC or 30,000 Satoshi.

Simple? Not really.

You see, if the price of one Bitcoin the very next day is US$8,500 and I go back for that same $3 coffee, then I've got to pay 0.00035294 BTC – 35,294 Satoshi. In other words, my coffee is now 17.65% more expensive for me to buy.

Now, that doesn't really work in the real world, does it?

That kind of volatility doesn't really fly for a "currency". At least with a US dollar, pound sterling or Aussie dollar you know that if you have one today, tomorrow it will still be worth one.

However... things get a little more complicated over time. Because over time, over a year or two even, that USD/GBP/AUD actually *isn't* worth one any more. Through the interference of governments and central banks, through inflation, that one will change in value over time as well.

The key difference is that it takes a lot longer for a current fiat one to change in value. Bitcoin, on the other hand, can swing wildly in value not just from month to month, but from day to day – heck, even hour to hour the price of Bitcoin can swing dramatically higher... and lower.

A more stable situation would be if the coffee cost, say, 100,000 Satoshi, rather than US$3. So when you walk in they expect you to pay in Bitcoin, not pay in Bitcoin that has to then be converted back to fiat currency.

And therein lies the problem. Bitcoin as a system works wonderfully *if you get complete buy in from an economy and an entire supply chain.* It's almost like the chicken and egg problem... one of them has to come first.

If you're constantly converting Bitcoin into and out of

fiat currency, then it's hard for merchants to justify the wild price swings that pose a risk to business. And you're then really just trying to bridge the new alternative crypto system to the existing flawed, broken, inefficient traditional financial system.

If the price of Bitcoin swings the other way and the value of one Bitcoin goes up, then that US$3 coffee becomes cheaper for me, and the coffee shop makes less money. That is, they get less Bitcoin for that coffee than they would have yesterday.

If merchants, employers and users all dropped the comparison to fiat currency, then perhaps we would start to see more stability in the price of Bitcoin. But that's hard when you're in this strange transition phase, when you're paid in and dealing in many different global currencies... while still trying to build a huge, comprehensive, global network and alternative financial system, with a separate, global digital currency.

And that's why my view is that, for now, Bitcoin isn't a currency at all. Instead, right now Bitcoin is a store of value rather than a currency. And later, in about 127 years' time, long after we're dead, it will become a currency that an entire supply chain can reliably use in all aspects of pricing, payment and acceptance.

That's the view I have on it right now. And I believe that Bitcoin will become a proper global currency where someone from Sudan can exchange and interact with Bitcoin as easily and efficiently as someone from Australia, the US, UK, Chile, India, Jamaica or Cambodia. That day where Bitcoin is widely accepted as a global reserve I think is actually coming very soon, perhaps within the next 10 years – but in terms of global trade and supply chains and the "alternative system" becoming the main one, that's going to take a lot longer.

Don't forget crypto is debasing a traditional system that's had a few hundred years head start on it.

But crucially, when you think of Bitcoin and its future, you need to shake free your preconceptions and comparisons to fiat currencies. Think about things in Bitcoin, not dollars or pounds. Even just try it for a day – and don't think about the value of anything in fiat currency.

Trust me, it's hard. But we'll get there eventually.

But that eventual use of Bitcoin as a currency may be some time away. As it evolves through to the complete mining and distribution of all Bitcoin, it will continue to exist as a store of value. As the overall network grows in size it inherently grows in value. And it's not until the network (the blockchain) is big enough, widespread enough and stable enough that the transition from store of value to currency will take place.

While I think we will easily be able to pay for goods and services in Bitcoin in 10 years, by then it will just sit alongside other fiat currencies. For Bitcoin to completely replace the current global financial system will take 100 years or more – and that's how generational wealth will be created.

And when that transition happens I believe it will coincide with the biggest event in the future of Bitcoin. When all 21 million coins that will ever be "mined" are in circulation.

Around the year 2140 all 20,999,999.97690000 BTC will be mined. And based on the current value of Bitcoin at the time of writing, around US$8,000, that would give the total Bitcoin network a (fiat comparative) value of just US$168 billion.

But the *real total circulation* of Bitcoin in the year 2140 will be 2,099,999,997,690,000 *Satoshi* in circulation.

That's 2.099 quadrillion Satoshi. Now, if you think about it as a widespread global payments system, and instead of talking in whole Bitcoin we consider the standard unit of Bitcoin as a Satoshi, things become very different.

US$56 billion doesn't even come close to the value of what that global network could be worth. Think about it like this...

That $3 cup of coffee might actually cost 3 Satoshi. And if that's the case, and a single Satoshi is worth the equivalent of 1 fiat US dollar, that would give the total Bitcoin network, the blockchain, a value of US$2.099 *quadrillion*.

If that's how it pans out – and in another 100 years I think that's exactly how it will pan out – then just one whole Bitcoin would be worth $100,000,000. This is what I mean by long-term, generational wealth.

And that's why now I think everyone should try to attempt to get at least one whole Bitcoin in the war chest, hold it, and pass it down through the next few generations; that decision may prove to be the best thing you'll ever do for you family's legacy.

Chapter 9: Our technological saviour – the blockchain

With a greater concept of Bitcoin itself, you must understand how the network value is created over time. And to do that, you must know what makes it work. And that's the Bitcoin network, its blockchain.

Bitcoin is one giant distributed network that exists online around the world. That's what gives it value. That's what makes it function. That is the blockchain.

Imagine if every financial transaction that has ever taken place in the world were to be recorded in one giant book. Imagine a huge notepad-style accountant's ledger.

In that ledger, if you buy that $3 cup of coffee the transaction is recorded. Then, when that coffee shop transfers the money at the end of the day into their bank account, that transaction is also recorded. Then when that money is used to pay staff wages, that too is recorded in the giant ledger. And if the money is spent to buy more coffee beans then – you guessed it – that transaction is also recorded.

Now imagine that you have the ability to read that ledger at any time you like. You can just pick it up and see all the transactions that have taken place at any second of any day over the history of all financial transactions. You can jump into that ledger and see the transaction that took place between you and the coffee shop. You can actually trace the origins and pathways of every one of those dollars, where it's been, and where it's gone since it first began life as a dollar.

Right there, etched in history, is the transfer of your US$3 to the coffee shop. You can see that it's accurate, and you confirm as such. There are also others that confirm this transaction. They might have been able to prove the movement of those dollars previously, and so do you, and then onwards from here.

And once there are enough people confirming these transactions, the whole network of people who can see this giant ledger give it the green light and it will exist forever, etched in history, that this transaction took place.

And this happens for *every transaction that ever takes place in history*.

Now imagine that process of transactions and confirmations happening for every single transaction that takes place every second of every day. In the world we live in, that's billions of transactions a day. It's immense. But the entire network validates the transfer and flow of money and transactions.

It's not reliant on a bank, clearing house or a payments messaging organisation. The peers on the network, the network itself, validates and confirms everything that happens, without interference of influence. This is a secure, peer-to-peer network operating a digital bookkeeping service – a distributed, public, digital ledger.

In the world we live in today, there's one slight catch with all this. Most people don't want the entire world to know about every transaction they make at any moment, or have it permanently etched in this giant ledger for all of history.

So imagine a situation where every one of those transactions – like that coffee you bought – was encrypted. So the people who verify the transaction can see that it took place, but don't know that it was you, and don't know it was at a coffee shop. All they can see is a digital identity. One that has no links to you, or to anything, because it's encrypted and anonymous.

That way, for every transaction that takes place, you can still see the flow of money. You can prove and verify the transactions taking place. But you never know who it's flowing from, or who it's flowing to. You just see a jumbled mess of letters and numbers (the encrypted transaction).

The added beauty of this is that, in order for it all to work and the transactions to take place, everyone that can see this giant ledger is able to confirm and validate transactions. Without a central authority. And it can be achieved with speed at low cost, while retaining the privacy of everyone who makes transactions.

In essence, this whole process of encrypted transactions is confirmed by the network of users, without a central authority, and is recorded on one giant all-encompassing ledger and this is the core system on which Bitcoin operates.

This is known as the blockchain.

The blockchain does what it says on the tin. It's a giant "chain" of "blocks", and it's these blocks that make up the ledger of all Bitcoin transactions that have ever taken place.

For example, the genesis Bitcoin "block" was mined (we'll get to mining shortly) back in 2009. This resulted in a 50 BTC reward for the miner (Nakamoto) who created it. Theoretically these Bitcoins that make up this genesis block get spent and transferred, and these transactions are recorded in each block. Every transaction has the time, date, the (encrypted) participants and amount recorded against it – a timestamp.

In order to confirm every transaction, "miners" (also known as nodes), solve complex mathematical algorithms automatically to ensure that every transaction, every block, adds to the previously confirmed blockchain.

Currently for a transaction to be added to the blockchain and approved, it must receive no fewer than six confirmations. If, for whatever reason, the block is fraudulent or inaccurate and isn't confirmed, it isn't added to the block – it is invalid and not processed. This process of confirmations is known as "proof of work" and is vital to ensure that transactions process, as well as preventing a situation of "double spend" from occurring.

Double spend is the idea that you can send Bitcoin in one transaction (so to pay for a coffee, for example) and before the transaction completes you spend that same Bitcoin again to buy something else.

By confirming transactions, you can't double spend. Or if you tried to, the network, the blockchain – and the nodes that confirm transaction – wouldn't validate the second transaction, and it wouldn't be added to the blockchain.

In order to confirm effectively every single transaction, *every single block must be able to be traced back to the genesis block.*

That means one huge, giant epic-beyond-proportions blockchain – but because of modern computing power and the relatively small size of the blocks, the actual process shouldn't theoretically take all that long.

However, there is a slight problem – and it comes back to the issue of scaling.

The bigger Bitcoin's blockchain gets, the bigger it gets (obviously). That means each block (measured in MB) adds to the blockchain, and the blockchain in total gets larger and harder to process. And eventually, to record all the transactions on every block as it all gets bigger, it simply slows down every-transaction, or there's a requirement that an ever increasing speed of hardware is needed to maintain processing speeds.

In other words, think of the blockchain as one giant linked chain piled up on the floor. When you lift the first link off the ground it's easy, and you can continue to lift the chain higher with speed and ease.

But as you lift it higher and higher into the air, the chain gets heavier in your hands. The higher you go, the more chain you now have to lift. When you're kilometres in the air that chain is so heavy that you can barely lift it any higher. You can still lift it up, but you're becoming steadily slower.

The only way to lift it as fast as you did with the first few links is to make it all lighter and easy to lift. And if you could make it so easy to lift that you could forever lift it as fast as the first few links of the chain, then I'm sure you would do that.

Well right now Bitcoin as a network is at the point where the chain is extremely heavy, and it's very slow to lift it any higher. It's also an expensive chain, where transaction costs get higher as the blockchain becomes more popular and more transactions take place.

And unless there is change, then the time taken to process

transactions will get too slow, until it becomes near on impossible to use. It will no longer be user-friendly. And certainly not acceptable for every-day, widespread use in the global crypto economy.

That means people will look to other alternatives outside of Bitcoin. Other cryptocurrencies to perform transactions in the digital and physical worlds. Faster ones, with less friction and with greater confidence.

This shows us that while Bitcoin has tremendous properties and is and will quite likely remain king long term, there are other cryptocurrencies there that hold potential to do what Bitcoin can't.

A scaling problem is a good problem to have. It shows progress and increasing adoption. However, it must be fixed, or if not fixed, then people need to appreciate the limitations of the blockchain it's based on.

To understand the problem a little deeper, you also need to understand why the blockchain gets so heavy to start with...

This "chain of blocks" is also known as a "hash". So for each and every new block, it must include a hash of the previous blocks. This is like having an accountant present at every single transaction that's ever taken place, to ensure that it's legitimate.

And as the Bitcoin network grows, so does its hash rate. And while hash rates are measured in trillions of hashes per second, the most important figure to understand about Bitcoin is its transactions per second.

As it stands, due to the original block size being 1MB, the Bitcoin blockchain can currently handle around *three to seven transactions per second.*

However, compare this to an existing global payments system like Visa. Visa can handle around 2,000 transactions per second. That puts Bitcoin some way behind the eight ball should it reach the masses around the world.

Realistically, a blockchain needs to handle numbers more like 100,000 per second, maybe even 1 million per second to be a true disruption to the major payments systems and companies that dominate the traditional global payments system.

Maybe Bitcoin gets there through innovation like the Lightning Network which holds the potential to use side-chains – like a parallel blockchain connected to Bitcoin's blockchain that can facilitate those speedy transactions.

Or maybe Bitcoin doesn't aim to end up as the ultimate in payments, and becomes the "digital gold" that many believe it has become, a real crypto store of value for larger wealth.

But if change is needed, it's not easy to implement. Due to the public nature of the blockchain and its widely distributed nature, the entire network confirms transactions and updates the blockchain automatically and continuously. If there is a fraudulent transaction or a corrupt transaction, then the widespread nodes will not agree on the transaction and it will be denied.

That also means changes and updates to the blockchain and system are approved or disapproved by the entire network, developers, nodes, miners, as a consensus. Without majority consensus, the changes don't happen.

While that makes for a free system, it also means decisions, important decisions, can take time, or be incredibly hard to push through. But ultimately, if consensus is reached, the entire network, the entire blockchain, benefits.

What is an interesting feature also is that if you decide that the direction of Bitcoin's blockchain isn't the right one, you can "fork" the blockchain, which means at a point in time you can use a new set of nodes to recognise code changes to the core protocols.

This in effect creates a new parallel, and now independent blockchain, which you can develop how you see fit.

These forks happen quite regularly. But the trick is getting the wider communities to accept that your new forked blockchain is better and to get them to accept yours as the dominant blockchain.

That's a hurdle no one has been able to cross. But what it does tell us is that you can almost treat forks like an experiment to see if there is a better way or a different way, and the better, more accepted outcome, the one that most people use and flock to, will end up as a successor.

We've now seen forks like Bitcoin Cash, Bitcoin SV, Bitcoin Gold, Bitcoin Private, Super Bitcoin... all forks from the Bitcoin blockchain, and while some are moderately successful, none have been able to replicate or surpass the strength of the original core Bitcoin.

This means that the current Bitcoin blockchain is ultimately the most trusted source. The whole system is self-checking and self-regulating. You can't defeat the power of mathematics and the distributed ledger system.

Blockchain is the revolutionary technology that is changing the global banking system. Bitcoin as a store of value get the headlines, but if you boil the entire cryptocurrency boom down to one single core technology, it's the blockchain.

While it's still the core, decentralised technology underpinning, Bitcoin, corporations, banks and governments are now experimenting with their own blockchain technologies for new ways to manage payments, transfer of assets, and how they shuffle fiat money around the world.

They're using new platforms to create private blockchains, and in some instances joining forces and creating alliances – as with the Ethereum platform – to see how they can take advantage of this technology.

While Bitcoin was and is the first, the number of crypto currencies looking to improve on it has exponentially increased. There are now thousands different kinds of cryptocurrency in the world. Many of them are based on Bitcoin's core code. Many of them have simply copied Bitcoin, hoping to reach the masses as well.

But many have created their own, unique blockchains, ones that do completely different things to Bitcoin. These other blockchains and the crypto that exist on them are also building out a crypto ecosystem that is rebuilding and creating new global networks and connections.

It's this crypto expanse that holds so much potential in creating a more equitable, global network. It's also wrestling power away from centralised authority and elites back to the individual, giving people greater control over their personal data, finances and overall lives.

But the Bitcoin blockchain (for now) remains strong, and is the most accepted and popular cryptocurrency in existence. It is working through its problems, and will come out the other side of it stronger.

The wider population is now seeing the potential of Bitcoin and blockchain technology. They now see how it can be used in the real world to fix a broken system.

Chapter 10: Mines, miners, a digital gold rush and claiming a stake

One of the critical infrastructures of Bitcoin and its blockchain are miners or nodes. A Bitcoin miner is a person or business that uses computing technology to mine Bitcoins. They also provide a secondary purpose in being a node on the blockchain. These nodes provide the automated process of confirming (or denying) transactions on the blockchain, enabling the entire Bitcoin system to function.

When you combine miners together they are an incredibly powerful aspect of the network. They also help to provide consensus for changes to the Bitcoin core code, or implementing changes to the network through "Bitcoin Improvement Proposals" (BIP).

But what is "mining" and how does it work?

The digital gold rush

To mine Bitcoin you need a computer – today an incredibly powerful computer, nothing like the ones you buy from the local computer store. No, the Bitcoin mining "rigs" today are more like supercomputers.

But in the early days of Bitcoin, if you had a home personal computer with a powerful GPUs, you could efficiently and effectively mine Bitcoin, and they would come flooding in.

Early on this meant that anyone with a bit of computer programming knowledge, a couple of Nvidia GPUs and some time on their hands could mint their own fortune.

Back in 2010 a humble home PC with a decent Nvidia GPU was all you really needed. The chance of mining a block of Bitcoin was actually pretty good. And if you got a block your reward was 50 Bitcoins – that's right, 50 Bitcoins.

Of course, back then that was worth maybe $20-$50. Not

the $400,000 it would be worth today!

Anyway, you still needed a high level of technical proficiency to get things up and running.

There were and still are miners that would mine Bitcoin with the sole aim to mine and sell the Bitcoin, bringing in a tidy little profit.

However, as they mine more blocks, there are fewer left to mine. This is part of the scarcity built into Bitcoin. And more miners on the network with more computing power mean it's harder to get a block.

Also, the design of the Bitcoin system specifies a finite number of coins that will ever be in circulation.

The total coins that will *ever be in circulation* is 21 million. Right now about 16 million are in circulation. And with every 210,000 blocks, the mining reward halves.

To mine a block, originally there was a reward of 50 Bitcoins. After the first 210,000 blocks (10.5 million coins) the reward dropped to 25 coins. After the next 210,000 blocks (5.25 million) the reward dropped to 12.5 coins. The reward is currently 12.5 coins. But after another 210,000, the reward will be 6.25 in roughly May 2020.Then it will drop to 3.175 BTC as a reward 210,000 blocks later, and so on until all coins are in circulation.

According to Bitcoin Wiki estimations, all Bitcoins will be in circulation by 7 May, 2140. So there's a while to go still.

But this halving of the reward reminds me of Zeno's paradox of Achilles and the tortoise…

> *Achilles is in a race against a tortoise. But he gives the tortoise a head start. Although Achilles is much faster than the tortoise, he can never catch it and overtake it. The reason being by the time Achilles has covered the distance of the head start, the tortoise has moved further ahead albeit perhaps by not as much.*

> *Then as Achilles covers the next gap, by that stage, even though the tortoise is slower, he has again moved further afield. Each time Achilles covers the gap,*

the tortoise has moved ahead, even if by only a tiny margin. As such Achilles can never catch the tortoise as no matter how many infinite times he catches up, the tortoise always moves slightly ahead.

Try explaining that to a primary school kid...

While Zeno's paradox isn't exactly like Bitcoin mining, it's close. Because even though the Bitcoin mining reward will halve, and halve and halve again until all Bitcoins are in circulation, even then the miners will still be needed to mine, as the system requires the algorithm to continuously be solved in order to maintain transactions, operate nodes and ensure the blockchain continues to run.

Ultimately even past the mining and circulation of all Bitcoins, there are infinite numbers of transactions that will exist on the blockchain. In order for that to infinitely continue, miners are needed to make it happen.

Now in theory that sounds complex. And it is. But in a practical sense it means that to mine, you need a mining rig. And back in the good old days that just meant any old PC with a GPU.

And to set up a rig in order to mine, you needed to set up your computer with a Bitcoin client (program) that runs continuously to solve a complex algorithm. The algorithm that Bitcoin uses is a cryptography hash known as the SHA-256, applied twice.

A hash takes a large amount of data (all previous blocks) and shrinks it down into a smaller hash value (256 bits). Each block's hash is a "wax seal" of all the blocks and transactions before it.

Now in order to mine a new block a miner has to solve this algorithm which, when you break it down, involves:

1. Collecting the hash from the previously discovered block (easy).

2. Collecting a list of potential blocks.

3. Calculating a potential hash for these potential blocks with a random number.

4. Repeating the calculation until the hash is more than the current difficulty level – in which case you've mined a block. If your calculation is less than the current difficulty level, you keep going until it's more.

It's worth noting that if someone else figures out the algorithm calculation and random number before you, then you all start over again for the next block.

In effect, whoever can solve the algorithm first and fastest gets the block. It's a genuine race between all the miners in existence to mine blocks for reward. The tricky thing is to mine effectively you need *immense* computing power.

As I said, earlier in the good old days you could get by with relatively simple computing power. This is because if you were the only miner in existence, the difficulty level would be low, and you would be able to mine with ease. So you wouldn't be in a high-stakes competition with other people to get your hands on a block.

Just like the Californian gold rush days of 1849, early miners were able to mine with ease and little competition, profiting handsomely. As the wider world became aware of the opportunity at stake, they flooded to the fields to mine. Soon enough competition was fierce, and the likelihood of mining that gold decreased.

The same happened to Bitcoin. As more miners flooded to the network, the difficulty in solving the algorithm increased. Eventually, a home PC with a high quality GPU or even a couple of GPUs just wasn't good enough any more.

So people quickly figured out if you can ram as many GPUs together as possible you can get even more computing power. And more computing power means a better chance of figuring out the algorithm and mining a block.

Then dedicated mining rigs came to market. These application-specific integrated circuits (ASICs) were pure computational machines specifically running the Bitcoin client just to mine blocks.

The home user no longer had a chance.

Then corporations popped up. Giant networks of servers and GPUs. Basically, supercomputers rolled into town. For someone at home wanting to mine Bitcoin, it was like taking a spade to the gold fields and competing with the likes of BHP Billiton or Rio Tinto with their multi-million dollar mining machinery. The little guy just didn't stand a chance any more.

But as you would expect, with even more computing power coming online to solve the algorithm, the difficulty continued to shoot higher.

And up until 2013 when Bitcoin really hit the mainstream consciousness and its price skyrocketed, the difficulty in mining Bitcoin was relatively easy.

At the start of 2013 Bitcoin's difficulty was at around 3,000,0000D (difficulty). This was considerably higher than at the start of 2012, when it was about 1,100,000D – about 2.7 times higher from 2012 to 2013.

But by the start of 2014 the difficulty was at 1,400,000,000D. That a 466-times increase in the mining difficulty. And at the time of writing the current Bitcoin difficulty stands at 678,000,000,000D.

As Bitcoin attracted more miners to the market – just like the Gold Rush – the difficulty in mining took off. Soon it simply wasn't enough for a recreational Bitcoin miner to compete. You needed serious hardware and serious backing.

Today there are mining pools. They "pool" the computational input from all their users, servers, ASICs, to help solve the algorithm and mine a block and then distribute the proceeds depending on each user's proportional input.

Many of the big boys of Bitcoin mining now operate their pools out of China. And we're seeing well-funded, public companies now setting up massive crypto mining farms all over the world.

That means you have no chance any more of mining Bitcoin on your own.

Sorry, the money tree is closed for you, at least in Bitcoin it is.

Also, as every 210,000 blocks the Bitcoin reward halves, miners do also end up in a decreasing sum game where you get less and less reward per block, but require increasing amounts of computational power in order to remain competitive against other miners. But because of the transaction fee reward, long term this still proves to be a financially viable enterprise, with widespread mass adoption and an exponentially larger blockchain and billions of users making billions of transactions.

But put simply, if you want to mine for Bitcoin, don't. Running a home PC with even the best consumer grade GPUs from Nvidia is simply not going to be enough to come close to mining a block any more.

In 2009, 2010, 2011, maybe even 2012 you had a chance – but those days are long gone. Opportunity missed. Trust me, I know all about missed opportunity (see the final chapter). So take my advice, mining is important to understand, but fruitless to undertake – unless you're a well-funded, deep-pocketed Chinese mining pool or a public company. Then maybe you could do OK.

I've focused on the mining of blocks here. But I should point out that the more important function of the miners is to operate as nodes.

Miners node best

Eventually all blocks will be mined, and as such it will no longer be profitable or necessary to mine Bitcoin, because you can't. So what incentive is there to keep miners in the network, operating as nodes?

That's where the Bitcoin fee structure and transaction reward comes into play...

In order to actually mine a block your computer has to solve an algorithm. If you're first to achieve it, your reward is the block. I think we've established that. And of course solving any kind of algorithm isn't easy. It's too much computational energy for a human brain.

So, as I've explained, you can only do it with a powerful computer.

Anyhow, once a miner is mining Bitcoin they also become nodes, verifying transactions. As I mentioned earlier, it's all done through computers and the use of GPUs, as they are able to process all the information much faster than typical central processing units (CPUs).

In order to ensure there are enough nodes on the system, there is incentive to operate and support the network. There is a reward given to miners of Bitcoin. When the system was in its infancy it was 50 Bitcoins per block they could mine. But there are also transaction fees paid to miners, to ensure that the entire system stays well-oiled and functioning.

Thus if a miner mines a block, not only do they get the Bitcoin reward, they also get all the transaction fees from the transaction information included within that block.

What's important to note is that a user – you, for instance – doesn't have to include a transaction fee when making a Bitcoin transaction. And if you do choose to add a fee, it can be as little or as high as you like.

However, if you don't have to add a fee, miners also don't have to process your transaction as a priority. They prioritise bigger fee transactions. This in effect also creates a natural market for transaction fees.

The idea is that transaction fees incentivise miners to continue to operate even after the last Bitcoin has been mined. And transaction fees increase relative to block size, scale and priority of transaction. Transaction fees might be relatively expensive now, but that's because of the scaling debate issues. In time, with scale and more users, the fees will theoretically fall as the market finds its feet.

As such, while the Bitcoin reward will halve every 210,000 blocks until all Bitcoins are in circulation, the idea is that transaction fees will make it still worthwhile for miners, as the potential transaction fee reward will outweigh the Bitcoin reward.

So when all Bitcoins are in circulation, it's important to know that miners will still mine – except the Bitcoin reward will be zero. Continuing the mining will keep the blockchain going. But while a miner who mines won't get any Bitcoin, if they are rewarded in transaction fees, then it's estimated the reward will be just as significant, if not more than it currently is from receiving Bitcoin as a block generation reward.

That means there will be a tipping point where the transaction fee reward is better than the Bitcoin reward of mining a block. And, surprisingly, that's estimated to occur well before all Bitcoins are mined.

In other words, this economic incentive scheme motivates miners to continue to mine, continue to keep the blockchain going, continue to operate as nodes, and ensure that the Bitcoin system continues to work as intended.

Scaling problems and the miners vote

However, all of this starts to become more complex when you take into account the problem of increasing difficulty, more Bitcoin users, more miners and the whole new global payments system that Bitcoin is becoming.

At the beginning, Bitcoin was fast, low cost and efficient. But that's when a few hundred thousand people were using it. Extrapolate that out to millions, tens of millions, billions of people, and things get a whole lot trickier.

The biggest problem facing Bitcoin now is scale.

That means as Bitcoin gets bigger and more popular and more people transact with it, the size of the network and difficulty will increase so much based on its current code that things will get slow. So slow and so expensive that it might not make economical sense any more to use Bitcoin. Instead, other cryptocurrencies may prove to be a more viable global unit of exchange, such as Litecoin or Dash.

Now, fair warning, this might get a little *more* complex as I explain what the scaling problem is in detail.

Let's get into it...

As you can probably tell, I'm incredibly bullish on Bitcoin. And I continue to maintain that position. I still believe that, long term, the purchasing power of Bitcoin will be multiple-times higher than it is now. I've even gone on record saying the cryptocurrency could reach a fiat value of US$50,000 per Bitcoin short term, and longer term I could be looking at a multi-trillion dollar, even quadrillion dollar alternative global financial system — in that case, Bitcoin could be as high as $10,000,000 per Bitcoin.

But it's going to be a bumpy road along the way.

What you also need to appreciate is that, while now ten years old, Bitcoin is still incredibly early stage. You should really look at Bitcoin like a brand new start-up. While it carries incredible potential, it comes with risk that you don't find in any other kind of investment market.

Part of this risk is due to the decentralised nature of the system. As there's no overseeing central power, the development of Bitcoin is left to its community and users – the miners (nodes). This is both good, and difficult.

And as I've explained, when something needs to change it needs to carry a consensus of the system in order to work. But what if there isn't a consensus? What if two halves of the Bitcoin community hold opposing views of the development?

Surely that spells trouble?

Well that's essentially the predicament Bitcoin had. There was division in the community, which was a risk to the value and validity of Bitcoin.

At the core of this division was the size of the blockchain.

As it stands, every "block" on the Bitcoin blockchain carries a size of 1MB. There's an argument within the Bitcoin community that the Bitcoin block size needs to be larger – 2MB or more.

The 1MB limit currently imposed on block size is arbitrary. It's just what Satoshi Nakamoto decided it should be when he created Bitcoin. The problem is that a 1MB limit restricts the transaction capacity of Bitcoin as it scales.

Still with me? Sorry if this is getting a little technical. I'll get to the crux of things in a moment.

The Bitcoin network is restricted to around seven transactions per second. For it to be widely used and accepted in the same way Visa or MasterCard are, that needs to be up in the hundreds of thousands, maybe millions of transactions per second.

This scalability came to a head as half the community wanted the blockchain to go through a "hard fork". And we touched on the forks earlier but this is why they came into existence and it's important to then understand some of the new blockchain solutions out there.

The idea was to hard fork the blockchain size to 2MB, and maybe more, to enable the scaling and mass adoption of Bitcoin. But it's not that simple.

Increasing the block size enhances the reward for being a miner on the blockchain. Transaction rewards remain high, as they require high-level computational power. Hence the driving force behind the hard fork was huge virtual mining companies.

There were and are other options to scale Bitcoin, aside from increasing the block size. That includes compressing the existing blocks, SegWit (which gets rid of unnecessary data in the transactions), or even adopting a Lightning Network, which sets up hubs that users primarily deal with and which occasionally settle on the blockchain.

Of course this doesn't factor in advances in computing power, speed, AI and ultimately quantum computing – in which case block size would be a completely redundant argument. And also in which anonymity and the cryptographic foundation of Bitcoin might become an issue.

But back to the issue at hand.

What this all boils down to is that when someone or some group decides Bitcoin needs to change, it goes through a hard fork and branches off into a whole separate blockchain.

This situation was a near civil war within the Bitcoin community when Bitcoin Cash forked from Bitcoin.

Now I want to emphasise, this infighting didn't kill Bitcoin and even Bitcoin Cash has a devout set of followers.

I'm of the view these forks will ultimately end up in a stronger, more widespread system.

Long term, Bitcoin's potential is as strong as it was yesterday. But we just don't know which version, which implementation of Bitcoin will be the ultimate winner. Maybe they all end up existing, just at varying adoption – and maybe one day there's a solution to bring them all back together, talking to or at least interoperable with one another in a seamless fashion.

That's the beauty of crypto, the development potential is nearly unfathomable as to what's possible over time.

But what we do know is that forks seem to be a natural evolutionary aspect of crypto blockchains as we try to work our way through what works and what doesn't.

And that's led to some incredible nifty potential solutions around how blockchains function, evolve and even reach a state of governance and consensus.

There's no denying the difficulty involved in trying to reach a consensus when you have a widespread distributed network. This is a *disadvantage* of a decentralised system. But when there is agreement and there's consensus then everyone wins, not just a few – and this is an advantage of a decentralised system.

A cryptocurrency and blockchain like Tezos (XTZ) for example is promising to deliver a "self-amending" blockchain. That means that the stakeholders on the network, token holders, validators and stakers are able to vote on changes to the Tezos blockchain.

By enabling everyone to have input and vote, once a quorum is achieved, then the process can start on improving the blockchain immediately.

In that sense the Tezos blockchain by design ultimately doesn't ever need to fork as the voting and governance system allows for improvement protocols to be implemented on what the network decides as a whole.

This novel approach to blockchain governance by Tezos is just one example of alternative approaches to how a blockchain can function and exist that's different to Bitcoin and other crypto, yet presents an equally compelling future value potential.

Mine or just set down your stake?

Now while Bitcoin's blockchain uses a process of mining to confirm blocks on its blockchain, there are other ways to prove blocks and secure a blockchain.

Mining and Bitcoin's proof-of-work blockchain is resource and energy intensive. But other crypto have developed and use a different method of consensus known as proof-of-stake.

The guiding principles of proof-of-stake is that validators on the network validate and confirm the blocks.

But instead of them implementing complex hardware mining, the algorithms for consensus are designed so that the "trust" of these validators is based on their stake of tokens on the network.

Hence big stakes on the network become more dominant block validators. Now the argument is that you actually have a greater risk of centralisation with proof-of-stake as there's potential for one massive stakeholder to effectively control the blockchain.

And in some situations that is the case, but that's often in crypto that aren't particularly decentralised to start with and where shady operation is prominent from the outset.

But there are a few crypto projects out there that

promise decentralisation, and can prove it where these large validators with huge token holdings are many, hence to command and conquer the network would be cost prohibitive and as difficult to achieve as attacking Bitcoin's blockchain by controlling all the mining rigs and hash rate.

Proof-of-stake also has a benefit to even small users that don't have enough tokens to become validators.

You see, let's say to be an effective node, a validator, you really need millions of tokens. That might be impossible if you've only got a few hundred bucks to put towards tokens.

But with proof-of-stake blockchains you can delegate your tokens to a validator. In that sense they pool tokens from huge numbers of smaller stakers to be a validator on the network.

What's important is that you never lose control of your tokens with this delegation model, you kind of rent them out to these validators who run the necessary hardware to remain online all the time and to responsibly and accurately secure the blockchain.

As a result of delegating your tokens to the validators, they receive block rewards when they sign and confirm blocks. That's a reward system like Bitcoin in that sense. But when a validator receives the reward for their work as a validator, they then distribute the proceeds out to the stakers that have delegated tokens to them, less operational fees.

For example, let's say you hold 5,000 tokens and you delegate them to validator A. Validator A is a good, strong reliable validator on the network. And with each block cycle that passes they get a reward.

Your stake of 5,000 then proportionally receives the reward the validator gets. And perhaps with this particular blockchain the average reward for a staker and delegator works out at 10% per year.

And let's say the rewards are paid out every three or four days. That means over the year you would expect around 500 tokens for delegating your stake. But as it's paid out every few days, you might end up with around a couple of new tokens every few days for simply delegating your stake.

This is a little bit like how stocks pay out dividends. Dividends are typically profits from a company that are distributed out to shareholders as a reward for being a shareholder.

With proof-of-stake, token holders are rewarded with new tokens for simply delegating their token stake, which helps to secure the blockchain they're based on.

And it means that depending on which blockchain proof-of-stake you're using, rewards can be a few per cent reward per year and we know of one crypto that's got a staking reward of more than 100% per year.

It all depends on the economics and structure of the crypto that's delivering the proof-of-stake consensus.

And what's making proof-of-stake so appealing is it's energy efficient, as it doesn't have the same immense hardware and energy reliance that proof-of-work like Bitcoin has, but also you can get payouts of crypto rewards for idly delegating your tokens.

If you couple that in with the potential for massive value appreciation in the tokens long term, then staking and delegating tokens for reward becomes a very attractive proposition.

That's why massive crypto exchanges like Coinbase are developing custodial services for massive institutional money offering up services like staking-as-a-service where they will hold and delegate or even operate a node and validator for big money clients and pay back the reward to them for delegation.

It's a huge growth area and opportunity in crypto and again demonstrates how fast and how advanced the ecosystem is getting. But also demonstrates that it's not just all about Bitcoin any more, but other huge alternative crypto as well.

And to make proof-of-stake even more solidified in the future of crypto, Ethereum, the world's second largest crypto by "market cap", is getting ever closer to migrating its proof-of-work consensus to a proof-of-stake one, which would be a massive catalyst for Ethereum and ETH tokens (which again, we'll get to shortly).

But proof-of-work, proof-of-stake is all well and well. The real question is how do you even get some crypto?

And the best place to start is the easiest one – how do you get your hands on some Bitcoin?

Chapter 11: Easy ways to get yourself some Bitcoin

Now you have an understanding of Bitcoin, its origins, its purpose, and its potential, how it works and some of the technical details behind it.

But the number one question I get on a daily basis is, "How do I buy Bitcoin?"

Here's how…

First off, let's remember this is a digital currency. A bank does not back it, it's not government protected. It is still inherently risky because with Bitcoin *you are your own bank*, and there's even risk you'll simply lose it.

I'll explain what to do next. But you must make sure you're aware that if you lose your digital wallet, send Bitcoin to a wrong address, forget how to access your wallet or are physically robbed and have them stolen, you may never recover them. You could lose every cent you put into it. That's high risk. But I think if you're careful and do things properly, methodically and carefully then you can minimise those risks.

I also suggest that you start off slowly. Set things up and buy a little bit of Bitcoin. Then get some more as you get more comfortable with the process. Maybe even hold them across multiple wallets to keep them segregated and safe and to spread some of those risks of holding.

By now you may be asking, what is a wallet? I'll let you in on a secret, this is actually not all that dissimilar to a wallet you might hold your cash and cards in… just that this one is digital.

This is the first step to getting Bitcoin. You need a "wallet". A Bitcoin wallet is a digital wallet where you store Bitcoin. Simple.

The best resource to get a wallet is on the Bitcoin. org website. In fact, you should use Bitcoin.org as a resource regularly to make sure you're comfortable with everything.

If you go to the link Bitcoin.org/en/choose-your-wallet you can find a wallet to store your Bitcoin.

There are a number of choices.

They range from wallets you can use on your mobile device to "web wallets", which are ones you can use on your computer and even "hardware wallets".

For what it's worth I've used all of the different kinds from mobile wallets to web wallets and hardware wallets.

There are advantages to each...

A mobile wallet can be handy if you're on the go and need access to your Bitcoin. This is simply an app you install on your iOS or Android-enabled device that will generate a Bitcoin wallet address that you can send, store and transact your Bitcoin with.

A web wallet is typically one that you would install on your computer like your Mac or Windows computer... or Linux. These are useful if you're perhaps frequently on the computer and you're looking to maybe trade Bitcoin so you can quickly and easily use it to send Bitcoin around.

A hardware wallet, however, I believe to be the smartest way to store your crypto. These hardware wallets mean your Bitcoin wallets are stored on a secured device that often requires a password and pin to get access. Also you can only access these hardware wallets when you connect them to the computer or your phone. When not in use they're "airgapped", meaning they're not connected to the internet, which adds a layer of security to them.

They are, in my view, the safest way to store Bitcoin long term. They're not 100% foolproof, but nothing is in Bitcoin. But in terms of the best option to store for the long term, my view is you should really be looking to get a hardware wallet.

Installing a wallet is as easy as installing any kind of program you can download online. Click and wait. Simple.

Or on your phone, go to your App store – iOS, Google Play, Windows... whatever that is (who uses Windows phones anymore?) – and install the Bitcoin wallet app.

These days there are loads of wallets and storage solutions you can use. The development in Bitcoin over the last 10 years has meant it's never been easier to get and then keep your Bitcoin.

But make note, installing a wallet is the first and most important thing to do. So let's dig a little deeper into that.

Once you've installed a wallet, open it up. Often you'll be given a set of security words that you typically store somewhere safe that enable you to recover your wallet in the event you lose access to it. This is often referred to as the "seed phrase".

You should keep the seed phrase for all of your wallets (including non-Bitcoin ones) super safe and secure. Because if anyone gets access to those, they can "restore" your wallet anywhere they like and potentially steal your Bitcoin.

That might sound really risky, but again, this is part of what happens when you become your own bank, the impetus is on you to ensure you maintain good security and safety.

You should also set some security for your wallet. That means a very difficult password with letters, numbers, capitals, and symbols, or where possible use two-factor authentication (2FA) and possibly biometrics as well, like a fingerprint, should something like your phone enable it.

With a wallet set up, you're ready to receive some Bitcoin. You will note in your wallet that you have a receiving address. This is made up of a bunch of randomly generated numbers and letters. It might look something like "3Kz1dQfF6q55ySTC1HXMJLWNoRY4WEbr7qx".

Some Bitcoin wallet addresses start with a 1, some start with a 3, the ones that start with a 3 are known as SegWit wallets which are a result of the debate on the upgrades and changes to the Bitcoin core protocols.

Many operations now use wallets with a 3, and are a preferred wallet of choice to use, it's most likely if you're setting up a new wallet it will start with a 3.

Anyway, this long string of numbers and letters is your public address. This is the address that the blockchain will show when you get some Bitcoin and when you send some Bitcoin. While "public" as you can see, there's no identifier in there to determine that you're the wallet holder.

The reason for the complexity is because Bitcoin also functions semi-anonymously. So while your transaction might be easily found on the blockchain, it would only appear as above. No name, no address, no personally identifiable information.

This is another exciting feature of Bitcoin. While not completely impossible, it's extremely difficult to track transactions to any one individual. This, as you can imagine, causes its fair share of headaches for government and regulators.

But remember, there's nothing illegal about owning Bitcoin.

And most government regulators and taxation departments still barely have any idea of how to treat it. For now that makes it extremely attractive to users while government and central bank try (pointlessly) to catch up.

But you should also make sure to check any current government and tax regulations in your jurisdictions to make sure you still sit on the right side of any potential tax treatments or jurisdictional rules.

At this point I'll also add that government and central banks are also a risk that you should think about at this juncture in Bitcoin's journey. Regulation and government interference is a risk for Bitcoin. The ruling hand of government doesn't like what it doesn't understand, doesn't control and can't tax.

We'll touch on this risk a little more. But know that they inherently don't like Bitcoin. But again, that's what makes it such a great alternative payment system – it's decentralised, it's semi-anonymous, it's borderless, and it doesn't need the input and interference of local banks, central banks or government.

Now, back to your digital wallet.

You know your receiving public address — you'll need this to receive Bitcoin. It's important in your first transaction – and any transaction – to make sure you get this address 100% right.

Now, time to buy some Bitcoin. At this point you will be required to pay fiat money in order to get Bitcoin. But once you're in the world of crypto, there's no turning back – you'll be addicted!

There are a huge amount of exchanges where you can now get Bitcoin. I've used a number of Bitcoin exchanges to buy and exchange Bitcoin over the years. Some are still going strong and have become massive companies like Coinbase, others have faded into insignificance and even gone bankrupt and failed like Mt. Gox, Cryptsy and Cryptopia.

Some that you can use today include Coinbase, Bittylicious, Cointree, Bit Trade Australia, Gemini, Bitpanda, CEX.io, Kraken, Bittrex, Poloniex, Binance, Exmo. They all have their positives and negatives.

But for beginners to the world of cryptocurrency, we find Coinbase is one of the more straightforward and simple ways of getting Bitcoin. We might add that Coinbase can have slightly higher trading fees and sometimes can be a little slow to add payment details to build up your allowable trading amounts.

But in my view, it's clearly one of the simplest ways to get Bitcoin for outright beginners. When you're more comfortable with everything, you might want to look at other exchanges. But you can use Coinbase on your computer and phone, and it's very good user experience.

You will, of course, need to pass account verification before they'll sell you Bitcoins. That means providing photo ID and typically the use of a mobile phone in order to receive a verification code to verify your account. And you'll need to use your *real details* to register.

Some (like Bittylicious) require that the account you pay for your Bitcoins in is the same name you register your account with – so no dodging this fact by using fake names. It's an unfortunate part of getting into crypto; you still have to exit the traditional fiat money system to enter crypto.

But as I say, once you're in, then you have far more ability to move your funds anywhere anytime without the prying eyes of central authorities.

Now, back to using Coinbase as an example. Once you've got a verified account with them, you simply enter how many Bitcoins you want or you enter how much in your local currency you want to spend.

Another point here. Coinbase also charges a service fee. And the smaller your purchase, the more relatively expensive the fee. It's steep, but that's the price you pay for one of the easiest ways to buy Bitcoin.

The good thing about Coinbase is that it accepts payments by most kinds of debit or credit card, and you can also pay via bank transfer. Again, as daunting as this might seem to start with, you must simply view it the same way you would view setting up a stocks trading account.

In fact, you'd have to jump through *more* hoops to buy and sell stocks than you do to buy and sell Bitcoin and other cryptocurrency. When you realise how easy it actually is and have just a modicum of patience with the setup and registration process, then you'll understand just how simple this world is to get involved in today.

With Coinbase, once you determine how much you want, you enter the amount in the buy/sell tab. And then buy your Bitcoin – easy!

What this will do is hold your Bitcoin in an automatically set up Bitcoin wallet in your Coinbase account.

But with some other sites you're required to enter a *receiving address* to get your Bitcoin. That's why you needed to set up a Bitcoin wallet to start with.

That's how it works on Bittylicious, for example. So when

you go to buy your Bitcoin off a site that doesn't set up a wallet for you, and in order to have your Bitcoin purchase sent somewhere, you need to have a Bitcoin wallet.

Get the details of your already set up Bitcoin wallet perfect when you're putting it into a recipient address. **This is _very important to get right._** You need to make sure you enter your wallet address *perfectly!*

If you get it wrong, your Bitcoin ends up going to someone else's wallet because you put in the wrong wallet address. And you're the only one to blame in that situation. You'll probably never see the Bitcoin or money again.

This is another reason why I say start with a small amount to get used to the process if this is your first time. Do not just send a huge chunk of Bitcoin in one hit if it's the first time you're sending to a particular wallet or into a new account. Test it out first to make sure it's sound, and then go with the rest.

I do this *every time* I set up a new account somewhere. For example, say I set up a new wallet after buying a new Ledger hardware device. If I buy from Coinbase I will maybe transfer 0.05 Bitcoin to my new Bitcoin wallet to start with. When it hits my Ledger wallet, then I know it's all correct and I'll transfer the rest in one go.

Remember, each transfer takes a transaction fee (to keep the miners well oiled) so don't do too many transfers. Be sure you know where and why you're sending your Bitcoin.

But once you send the Bitcoin, wait, complete the transfer, complete the transaction, and after a bit of time (depending on the Bitcoin blockchain congestion) your Bitcoin will appear in your wallet.

At this point a lot of people get worried because the Bitcoin is no longer in their wallet, but not in the new wallet address either. That's because it's working its way through the blockchain, getting confirmations from the nodes verifying it's a valid transaction.

You can also always check your transaction (you'll always get a transaction reference ID) on the blockchain through sites like blockexplorer.com or blockchain.info.

You will then see the transaction and the number of confirmations (or lack of) as it processes through the blockchain. If it's showing no confirmations, don't worry, it will happen. It's just that these days, Bitcoin transactions take a little longer than they used to, but remember we're here for the long haul, so a few extra minutes, maybe even 30 minutes or a couple of hours isn't anything to worry about if everything is showing on the blockchain.

The time it takes is getting longer than the early days. That's because of a number of factors including the sheer increase in size and number of people now using Bitcoin, but also the size of the Bitcoin "blocks".

This does mean that sending Bitcoin from one wallet to another or to an exchange can take as long as a couple of hours to move through. That's not overly efficient and that's why one of the most contentious topics in Bitcoin right now is the ability for it to scale. And that's why there are now so many different forks of Bitcoin.

But rest assured, when your transaction is in the blockchain and you got your addresses 100% right, then you will absolutely get those Bitcoins in your wallet.

And that's one of the great things about it all. You can see every step of the way where your Bitcoin has come from, gone to and ended up, thanks to the distributed ledger of the blockchain.

Again, don't worry when your purchasing wallet (on Coinbase for instance) and your receiving address (on blockchain.info for instance) both show 0 BTC. It's coming, just be patient.

So that's it. It's a pretty straightforward process these days. If only it was this easy back in 2011...

Now, you can set up any number of Bitcoin wallets. They're free to set up and you can do it on your computer, tablet, smartphone... any digital device, really.

You could hold different wallets for different purposes. One to invest, one to trade, one for the kids, one for the grandkids. Maybe even a secret stash for that boat you always dreamed of...

However you decide to set it up, once you've got your Bitcoin in your wallet the next most important thing you need to do is protect them. And that's why now you need to learn how to keep your investment safe from those who want it and will do almost anything to get it.

Chapter 12: Risk mitigation: how to store and secure your Bitcoin

In 2014 I was a guest on *The Rick Amato Show* on the US TV network One America News Network. I was there to talk about Bitcoin.

The main reason I was there in the first place was because of the recent (at the time) example of bankruptcy and fraud from a Bitcoin exchange, Mt. Gox.

Mt.Gox was the world's biggest Bitcoin exchange. It was handling around 70% of all Bitcoin transactions worldwide. It was huge! And many people, like me, fell victim to it.

On 14 February 2014 Mt. Gox simply vanished. Users couldn't log into the site. There was nothing anyone could do.

No one really knew what was going on. But what was clearly evident was that anyone who had Bitcoin or any other altcoin on the exchange was now missing their coins.

Eventually it came to light the exchange had declared bankruptcy. And over 744,000 BTC went "missing", worth roughly over US$400 million. I had a small amount of Bitcoin in a Mt. Gox wallet. Mine wasn't anything too dramatic to cry about at the time, all up it was about 0.1 BTC not heaps, but enough to want back!

But it just vanished, along with that of others who held far more than I did. The failing of Mt. Gox teaches us a valuable lesson about the world of Bitcoin – *if you don't control your private key, then you really don't control the safety of your Bitcoin*.

A popular saying amongst the crypto community is, "not your keys, not your crypto".

Another example of a failed exchange was the demise of Cryptsy, another cryptocurrency exchange. One day, it too suddenly disappeared. Users couldn't log into accounts, and any and all Bitcoin or cryptocurrency that existed in Cryptsy accounts went missing.

Without access to private keys, users had no way of accessing their crypto or getting it out. And to this day, most people still don't have it. There is a class-action lawsuit against Cryptsy, but the chances of getting anything back are remote.

This is the problem with "hot wallets" which are continuously connected and accessible online and that are often used by exchanges. It's what happens when your wallet is held by a third party, such as Coinbase, Bittrex, Poloniex, Livecoin, or any exchange or third party running a hot wallet. They control the private keys, not you.

So if they go bankrupt, decide to just make off with all the funds or do something that cleans you out of your crypto, there's not a lot you can do.

We've even seen more recent examples of this play out with hacks on major exchanges like Binance, the hack on New Zealand's Cryptopia exchange and the weird story of the disappearance of users' crypto from Canadian exchange, Quadriga.

I've seen my own Bitcoin and crypto on Mt. Gox and Crypsty disappear. You simply have to live with the fact that you weren't secure enough with your crypto. But you can learn from these examples and from mistakes of those like me who have been around this space long enough.

The most important lesson from my Mt. Gox and Cryptsy episode was to make sure that you store your Bitcoin and crypto in a safe and secure way.

But let's focus on Bitcoin here, because at the end of the day it's the easiest to store safely. And anyway, plenty of other cryptos like Ethereum, Ripple, Dash and Litecoin are able to be sorted exactly the same way.

So if you can get it right with Bitcoin, you can pretty much get it right with any crypto.

Albeit for some people, this is still a laborious and challenging task. But the good news is that it's so much easier today than it was six or seven years ago.

That is, even for someone with a high level of technical prowess, getting and storing Bitcoin in 2010 wasn't as easy as you'd think. For people with coding and programming background it was reasonably straightforward but for a humble financial adviser (at the time) it wasn't all so easy.

But now, with update years of research and experimentation and doing it all myself, I'm happy to say not only is it easier to store, but it's safer than ever. And in the next couple of years it will get easier again.

But be persistent now and you'll come to thank me later!

Today there are specific hardware devices you can buy that let you keep your Bitcoin and other cryptocurrency completely offline, as I say, they're "airgapped" so they're not vulnerable at all to digital attackers while offline – note: they are still vulnerable to physical theft.

Now before you go another step further, there's another thing to consider. You need to figure out *what you want to do with your Bitcoin.*

For example, if you're buying Bitcoin with a long-term goal of holding them anticipating an appreciation in purchasing power, then get your Bitcoin off the exchange, and get it out of the third-party application, get it into a hardware wallet, nice and secure.

That means transferring it into a wallet that exists offline.

However, if you're holding Bitcoin or any other cryptocurrency to actively trade in and out of different crypto, then holding it all in cold storage isn't practical. Not only does it then take time to get your crypto from the wallet to the exchange (potentially missing out on trade opportunities) but you also chip away at your store of value through ongoing transaction fees.

As I say, if you're trading then you'll need to just keep your trading coins in a wallet with fast access. In extreme cases you can keep them on the exchange, but I'd consider this a last resort.

For speed, ease of access and a decent element of security a mobile wallet is likely your best bet if you want to quickly have access to crypto without carrying around your hardware wallets everywhere.

But let's look a little deeper at each option.

First up, cold storage, or hardware wallets.

I absolutely recommend that you get a hardware wallet device. Trezor, Ledger, KeepKey, OpenDime are all examples of quality hardware wallets. Personally, I use a number of Ledger and Trezor devices for my long-term crypto holdings.

I use a Ledger Nano S. It's very easy to set up and you can store Bitcoin, Ethereum, Ripple, Litecoin, Dash, Zcash and Dogecoin on it. More and more crypto are added to compatibility for these hardware wallets all the time.

Ledger also makes a number of different devices, as does Trezor. When you head to their websites you'll find one that's most suitable for your needs.

Ledger even has connectivity kits to let you connect your ledger device to your mobile phone, so you can still access your crypto from your hardware wallet on your phone anywhere, anytime – that's a huge development of recent times, making their hardware wallets much more portable and user-friendly.

The way these cold storage hardware wallets work is they have the wallet, public and private key all on the storage device. You plug it into your computer or phone to load it up with your Bitcoin, and then you disconnect it from your computer or phone.

There's no possible way anyone can get at your wallet while disconnected. It's separate and not connected. And your private key is safely tucked away, too.

Of course the risk this then presents is the physical risk of losing, accidentally destroying or having your hardware device physically stolen. In that sense most of them come with a 12 to 24-word recovery phrase that is also needed to recover the wallet in the event of one of those disastrous events.

And if you lose those phrases as well, then you're in trouble. Then there's no way to recover your wallet. So it's important you know where and how to get your hardware wallet at all times. It might even be worth keeping it in a safety deposit box or some kind of secure safe or vault, if you've got enough on there. I like the safety deposit box idea because, again, that's what I do.

Also you can use devices like Billfodl that enable you to store your secret seed phrases on a metal device that's fireproof and virtually indestructible.

But in my view, the safest way to store your Bitcoin long term is by using one of these hardware wallet cold storage devices. I do it myself, and I advise you do the same.

Now you will also see that in purchasing these wallets it'll cost you some money to get one. The prices will eventually come down and there will be more options on the market. But for now, Trezor and Ledger are the two best in my view – and I have no affiliation with either, it's just based on personal experiences. Also it's the best investment you'll make to operate in a safer way in the world of crypto.

Also, because of the huge demand for Bitcoin and cryptocurrency, these are often out of stock. You can see months in delays before actually getting one.

In that case, there's only one thing to do – set up a wallet online.

While not as completely safe as a cold storage device, it's still a common and reasonably safe way to keep Bitcoin. Although it's probably best not to keep all your Bitcoins in one single wallet if you're building up a serious investment amount.

Here's how to set up an online wallet...

Ideally you want to set up a wallet with Blockchain. This is after all one of the easiest Bitcoin wallets to set up. And, again, one that I have used personally. You first need to register a wallet on the website. You do this by simply going to the site, clicking on "wallet" and then clicking on "create your wallet".

You enter an email address and a password and that's it, you have a Bitcoin wallet.

With the online wallet set up, you can easily transfer your Bitcoin in. But, again, just make sure you keep a record of all the important details like your wallet ID and password, because if you can't get into your wallet you can't get your Bitcoin.

Remember, this isn't like the bank. You can't just pop into a branch with multiple forms of ID to reactivate your account. Some wallet providers do provide supports that can help you get back into your wallet, but it's far more difficult to recover lost wallets than the traditional financial system.

This is, of course, a risk of Bitcoin and cryptocurrency – but also why it's growing in popularity. Because it can actually be even more safe and secure than your existing traditional financial system money.

And then I'd also classify a mobile wallet as an online wallet too. Doing it on your phone does enable security like a fingerprint reader, so people can't get into your phone physically. But again, remember, your phone is often a portal for potential cyber-attack, so it's also not always going to be the safest option either, but use strong passwords, 2FA and pin codes wherever you can.

Also more recently, mobile phone makers like HTC and Samsung have begun to get on board with crypto. They've been designing and building new phones with secure elements that enable the creation and security of crypto wallets on the device. HTC's Exodus in particular is a blockchain and crypto-specific device that could become hugely popular in crypto circles.

So that's it, it's not too hard to set up a wallet online.

The third and final option that suits people is to simply have a wallet set up on an exchange so you can trade in and out of Bitcoin regularly and quickly.

This is the easiest to set up. All you have to do is register an account on an exchange. Most exchanges only require an email address to get started. Then in the "balances" section of your exchange account you will find a whole heap of different wallets for different cryptocurrencies.

That means you can set up an exchange account under any name and any email address you have access to. But as you would expect, because it's so easy to set up, it's also the least secure.

While most exchanges have multiple points of security like 2FA, at the end of the day you are subject to the ongoing viability of the exchange you hold your crypto in.

And as I've seen first hand, if an exchange goes under, quite often so does all the crypto held there, too. So again, this really should be a last resort. Trust no exchange, ever.

Remember, they hold the private keys, not you, so that is a risk. And that's why I tend not to keep crypto on any one exchange any longer than is absolutely necessary, because if it did all go under then I wouldn't be too dramatically out of pocket.

Although, in times of incredible demand when the prices are flying and hype is building they can sometimes suffer from overloaded servers, slowing down access and preventing entry and exit to positions. Again, this is more a temporary problem that an outright concern about the exchange's viability.

Of course, nothing is ever 100% safe. However, just like stocks, bonds or even your traditional cash in the bank, anything can be stolen. The government steals your cash all the time through taxes. At least through cryptocurrency you can store your wealth in a protected, anonymous way that keeps it out of the hands of those that want to take it from you.

With the right safety measures in place, you can do your best to mitigate these risks.

Chapter 13: Now you've got it, how to spend or sell your Bitcoin

I've covered how to buy Bitcoin, how to protect Bitcoin. But another question I regularly get is, then what?

What do I do with my Bitcoin? Will I ever be able to use it? What's the point of it all? If it's for investment, don't I then have to sell it back to fiat currency at some point?

Well, at the risk of repeating myself, my view is that buying Bitcoin now is to speculate on it as a store of wealth so that in the future it will be worth considerably more.

I've always stood by the belief that once you own Bitcoin, you'll never need convert it back to fiat currency ever again. That's my view, that's the target I'm setting, and that's what I've always recommended.

For example, let's say one Bitcoin is worth US$8,000 today. My view is that in five to 10 years that Bitcoin could be worth (comparative to fiat US dollars) $100,000, $500,000, $1 million or, a few generations from now, the modern comparative equivalent of $100 million.

Now, again, I refer to it in dollars because that would be its *equivalent purchasing power* that people are used to and it's a reference most people can understand.

But the more accurate description would be to say...

If one Bitcoin can purchase a reasonable second-hand car, in five to 10 years' time, that one Bitcoin might be able to buy you a new Porsche or Bentley... or longer out maybe even a luxury boat... or even a house.

So the aim is that its long-term purchasing power will increase as the Bitcoin blockchain, the overall network, spreads and propagates around the world. Enabling access to its borderless, seamless system all over the world, to billions of people.

If that's the reach Bitcoin can achieve, then the inherent value of the network will be exponentially bigger than it is today. And in my analysis, that makes one Bitcoin worth more later than today. Network effect and Bitcoin's natural hedge against financial system crisis make it one of the most important new asset classes of the 21st century – perhaps of all time.

Also, as the network grows more and more, merchants will begin to accept it as a form of payment for goods and services.

For example, today you can use Bitcoin to pay household bills like school fees, electricity and gas. In Australia the Bitcoin payment processor livingroomofsatoshi.com allows for this.

And in 2017 it let the world know that it had processed over AU$5 million worth of Bitcoin bill payments – so people are clearly using Bitcoin in the real world today.

Also, recently companies like Amazon-owned Whole Foods and Starbucks have also started accepting crypto. Heck, I've even paid for some CBD vape refills online from Medipen in Bitcoin.

Now while you might be able to pay for a year of school fees with one Bitcoin today, or a Mocha-frappa-latte with a fraction of a Bitcoin, in another five years' time you might be able to pay for your child's *entire primary, secondary and tertiary education* with one Bitcoin. Or buy a lifetime supply of Starbucks coffees.

Or, in the coming future, car dealerships, real estate agents and major retailers will accept Bitcoin as a method of payment for goods and services.

So the question of "What can I do with my Bitcoin?" is actually quite simple to answer. You spend it. You can invest in it today with the view to spending it in the future. Or you can save it, store it and use it as a gift for future generations to come – maybe thinking of it as generational wealth planning.

In the same way you invest in stocks and property today so that at some point in the future you can use the profit proceeds to live a little, spend a little and do all the things you want to enjoy your life, well, the same will be able to be done with Bitcoin.

Investing in it now, while it's growing as a store of value, ultimately relates to using that same Bitcoin in the future to spend in the global economy. Except the global economy of the future won't be powered by multiple fiat currencies issued and manipulated by central banks and government. It will be decentralised, free from interference. It will be a global financial system powered by cryptocurrency and blockchain technology. It will be a crypto economy.

Of course, not everyone has that kind of long-term view or vantage point.

And not everyone shares my view on its long-term purchasing power potential or the widespread nature that Bitcoin will achieve. Some people just want to invest now and cash out short term to realise some profits in fiat money.

If that's your prerogative, that's fine. And the good news is it's just as easy to sell Bitcoin back into fiat money as it is to buy it with fiat money.

Now I will reiterate, the whole point here is to exit that traditional global banking and financial system. It's to get money into the crypto economy and then use it in that world – and in the real world.

So the aim, in my view is *not* to convert it back to fiat currency in the future but to utilise this new alternative financial system with Bitcoin and a whole range of other crypto and escape the constraints of our current system.

But if you must convert it back to fiat money, then you simply reverse the steps you take in buying Bitcoin.

For example, the major Bitcoin sellers I talked about before also enable you to sell your Bitcoin. Sometimes they buy them, sometimes they simply match you with new buyers of Bitcoin, like a P2P Bitcoin market.

With Bittylicious that's how it works. You jump on to its site and instead of choosing to buy Bitcoin, you choose to sell it. You'll then be given the details of how much to sell, what rate you'll get and the wallet address you need to send it to. You are also asked for the bank details you want the funds transferred to.

It all happens very quickly and securely, and lets you cash out of your Bitcoin.

The same is said for Coinbase. Except here you need to have your Bitcoin in your Coinbase account. So you'll need to transfer it in. Then when it's in your Coinbase account, you choose "sell" and sell your Bitcoin.

It really is as easy as buying or selling stocks through an online broking account.

Now what about a little more detail on how to spend it in the real world today?

In the early days there was little you could actually buy with Bitcoin. As explained in the 64 key moments that shaped Bitcoin, user Laszlo Hanyecz spent 10,000 Bitcoins on a pizza delivery. While not exactly the most economical decision, it was still an example of using Bitcoin in the real world.

And there are plenty of "meetups" around the world where Bitcoin users can exchange goods for Bitcoin in person – just like a car boot sale or Sunday market.

But there are many more avenues online to use Bitcoin to purchase real goods. As I've explained, livingroomofsatoshi.com in Australia allows for Bitcoin holders to pay for bills with Bitcoin.

That includes school fees, electricity and gas bills. Anything that you can BPAY (an electronic banking bill payment) you can use Bitcoin to pay. Credit card bill? Use Bitcoin. Mobile phone bill? Use Bitcoin.

What else can you buy now with Bitcoin? Well, if you head to overstock.com, a huge online marketplace, you can use Bitcoin to buy anything from its website too. Household goods, bedding, furniture, jewellery, watches, can all be purchased using Bitcoin.

It's just like any other payment method, as you check out with your basket and simply choose to pay with Bitcoin.

These are just a couple of examples of progressive businesses allowing people to pay with Bitcoin. And as we head into the next five,10 years, I anticipate that more companies like Overstock will begin accepting Bitcoin as a legitimate payment method.

And when a company like Amazon or Apple says they'll accept it, then watch the real explosion in Bitcoin prices as people all over the world begin to fully appreciate the potential to use Bitcoin for everyday items.

There are also companies like BitPay that help companies accept Bitcoin as payment for goods. An example of this from 2017 was reported in Bitcoin Magazine, and it shows that not only can Bitcoin be used for major purposes, but it can also inadvertently lead to other financial gain.

"We got approached last month by a real estate developer," Singh told Bloomberg Markets. "He had an offer to buy a house, and the purchaser wanted to pay in Bitcoin. And they weren't really sure what that was, so they contacted us."

Singh noted that Bitpay has helped facilitate these sorts of transactions several times over the past few years. "We walked him through how it works and the process," said Singh.

The purchase price of the home in question was roughly $4 million.

Singh went on to explain that the Bitcoin price was at $750 when the transaction to purchase the house was initiated. By the end of the transaction, the Bitcoin price was $1000. "So the buyer actually ended up making about 25 per cent in the currency exchange rate, essentially, in the appreciation," said Singh.

According to the numbers provided by Singh, the buyer of the home was left with an extra $1.3 million after the purchase of the home.

"With that extra money, he went and bought a Lamborghini at Newport Beach, Orange County, which also accepts Bitcoin with Bitpay," added Singh. "He got a house for pretty much 25 per cent cheaper, as well as a free Lamborghini essentially."

We see this kind of instance – real estate developers and agents accepting Bitcoin – as a more common occurrence. And should the price of Bitcoin continue to rise over the next five, 10, 20 years, it will absolutely take off.

Ultimately as Bitcoin becomes a widespread, mass-adopted unit of exchange, it will be as common to pay with Bitcoin as it currently is with a debit or credit card.

With that point also comes recent advances in cryptocurrency technology to allow for purchases in the real world.

There are a raft of companies, Wirex, Coinbase and a huge list of start-up-style crypto payments companies, that are all launching payment cards that you load up with your cryptocurrency and then use in the real world like you would a debit card.

So think about going into a shop – any retail shop – to buy some clothes. Instead of using your debit card you use your "crypto card". And instead of debiting your bank account in dollars, pounds or yuan, it debits your crypto wallet – taking a little bit of every crypto you have on there, proportionally.

You could load your crypto card wallet with Bitcoin, Litecoin, Dash and Pivx then when you pay in store for your goods, a little fraction of each gets taken as payment, converted to fiat money and then used as the payment unit of exchange to the retailer.

In fact, in one instance I was in Dubai airport and had some Bitcoin on my Wirex card. I decided to test it out and purchased a cheeseburger and a coke from McDonald's using my Wirex card, paying in Bitcoin.

These incredible innovations allow for real world use of Bitcoin and cryptocurrency. Something that simply didn't exist even just a few years ago. And much of the reason these kinds of crypto payment functions now exist is actually not necessarily just because of Bitcoin, it's due to other crypto like Ethereum. But we'll get to that shortly.

Chapter 14: Massive potential or massive hype? The future of Bitcoin

In late 2013, when Bitcoin hit an equivalent price of US$1,242, the world stood up and took notice. The same day Bitcoin hit US$1,242 the spot price for physical gold was US$1,240. This digital currency was worth more than gold. For many it was digital gold.

And then it fell off the radar. But governments and central banks went on their merry way racking up more and more debt – adding to the debt pile that future generations will have to pay off. There will be kids born this year, the year after and the decade after, that will have to pay off the debt that your government racks up today.

Imagine that. Imagine being born into debt that you didn't accrue. That's the situation today. We all have to pay it off. But we didn't ask for it, the government and central banks did it because they chose to; because they're the central authority.

But with crypto, the world gets another chance to impact their own financial future. Independent, decentralised and free from government and central bank control.

It's a true financial revolution. Even more, it's a social revolution that's been bubbling away under the surface since the 1980s really. One that only came to a head in 2008/09, and only now is starting to find its feet, begin to mature and open up the world to its full potential.

And that means an exciting future.

My position was, and still is, that Bitcoin will be around far longer than you or I will be alive. In fact, I don't envisage a day in the future, ever, when there isn't Bitcoin. Considering all coins won't even be in circulation until 2140, that's a good indication of its longevity.

When I was on *The Rick Amato Show* in 2014 talking about Bitcoin, while the other guest was laughing at me and saying Bitcoin was as valuable as "bubble-gum wrappers" and that it would be around by the end of the year (this was 2014 remember) I was saying to them that Bitcoin would outlive all of us and generations to come.

Bitcoin is, and always has been, a unit of exchange over the internet. It is, in its purest form, anti-government, anti-central bank. It provides the perfect basis of an alternative payment system. And no one can take it down, it's going to be around, in my view, forever.

I'm also of the view that the converted fiat currency value of Bitcoin is *unimportant* for the future. It matters little long term what Bitcoin is worth in USD, CNY, AUD, GBP or whatever currency you choose. One day you will be able to freely spend Bitcoin as you do today, with the currency you're paid your wages in.

But you'll be paid in Bitcoin. You will be able to work anywhere, for anyone, and have a universal currency. Supply chains will be priced in Bitcoin. Bitcoin will be a true universal currency, "the internet's currency".

There is, of course more economic considerations down the track about the value of goods and services from one country to the next. But crypto-economics is something else entirely, which we're still just trying to figure out.

However, there is a transition period to this day of global adoption when the fiat value will be important, giving us perspective as to the purchasing power of Bitcoin. For example, while the current price of Bitcoin is US$8,000, long term I can see it being the equivalent of US$50,000, and possibly US$1 million.

Let's see how that's possible.

Well, for a start we know if there will only ever be (just under) 21 million Bitcoin in circulation, you can start to get an idea if you think about it as a full global financial system.

In 2015 the World Economic Forum put out a research paper about critical events that could have enormous societal impact.

One of those it expects is that by 2027, 10% of global GDP will be stored on blockchain technology.

The OECD expects world GDP to surpass US$101 trillion by 2027. Now if 10% of that is stored on blockchain technology, that would make the crypto economy worth around US$11 trillion.

And let's assume that Bitcoin remains the pre-eminent store of wealth of blockchain technology as a unit of exchange in the future. But even, let's say if Bitcoin is just 30% of the total global blockchain technologies holding that global GDP that would make the Bitcoin network effectively worth US$3.3 trillion. Note: right now Bitcoin's "dominance" in terms of market capitalisation compared to all other crypto is over 50%.

Now by 2027 there will roughly 20 million Bitcoin in circulation.

The easy maths then tells us that, at that size, one Bitcoin would be worth around US$157,142.

And remember that's if Bitcoin is just 30% of the global blockchain technologies, which hold 10% of the world's GDP. And that's under the assumption there are 20 million accessible Bitcoins.

So you have to ask, if you're looking at raw future purchasing power and one Bitcoin is worth US$8,000 today, and could be worth as much as US$150,000 in the next eight years, is it expensive today or a bargain?

You should also consider that there are potentially millions of Bitcoins that are lost or sitting in wallets where people have forgotten about them, lost the access credentials needed to access them, or the adding up of immoveable Bitcoin crumbs in millions of wallets around the world.

The reality is that circulating Bitcoin will be probably closer to 18 million by 2027, which only adds to the potential purchasing power of a single, whole Bitcoin.

Of course, to get to that kind of price point and purchasing power (or more) there's the long road ahead. But it's the trajectory Bitcoin is on now.

Or there is a fast route, which could see it hit that kind of price appreciation even sooner.

The likelihood of that six-figure outcome coming sooner than eight years is enhanced if we continue to see more severe, ongoing financial turmoil in economies around the world, and if Bitcoin continues to repeat the previous cycles it's showed leading into and after the last two block reward halvings.

In terms of the potential based on global geopolitical risk, as I said before, it's the perfect alternative payment system. Imagine what could happen if there is a collapse of the current global financial system. If there is another major global financial debt crisis or more "Trump shock" in countries like France, Germany, Austria, the UK and Australia.

What if Russia goes to war? What if China goes to war in the South China Sea? What if the US finds a way to go to another war? What happens if the EU disbands and the euro falls apart, pushing countries back to currencies like the guilder, lira, franc, drachma, Deutsche mark and peseta?

When that happens I'd expect there will be a flight of wealth to Bitcoin. People now know that in times of turmoil, one of the safest places you could shift money is out and away from government oversight. And that maybe the crypto economy is a smarter way to store value.

One of the precursors to the immense year Bitcoin had in 2013 was the Greek debt crisis and Cypriot debt crisis in Europe. Furthermore, there was increased awareness and acceptance in China, as well as ongoing global recognition because of the immense rise in price.

Another debt crisis on a scale even bigger than Cyprus or Greece could send Bitcoin's price soaring again. Complete financial system collapse would likely see it peak and rise with the same (if not more) ferocity as it did in 2013.

What's different this time around is that we're not starting from a base of a few hundred dollars in comparative value, we're already talking thousands of dollars in comparative value. An exponential rise from here changes *everything*.

But remember, my view here isn't to just get Bitcoin with the aim of selling it back into fiat currency. While you can do that if you choose, my view has and always will be to hold it long term. One day you will be able to use it anywhere, and your purchasing power then should be substantially higher than it is today.

Even if there isn't global financial collapse, I still envisage more and more citizens from countries all over the world turning to Bitcoin, and the blockchain technology it's founded on, to manage global and local payments and exchanges for goods and services.

I could go on and on, but the point is that Bitcoin today has come off the hype and hysteria of 2013. It bottomed, it stabilised, and it's seeing more recognition and acceptance globally as a viable system. It's now achieved a degree of stability in price – although, to many, it's still too volatile.

That puts it in a strong position for investment. But again, the aim is investment with the view to use it to exchange in the future for far more than what you can get it for today. The idea is not to transfer it back to fiat currency.

Of course, the choice is yours.

I will say it one more time, though. I don't think you should look at Bitcoin as a way for easy short-term money. The aim isn't to buy Bitcoin to sell back into fiat currency. The aim is that Bitcoin will continue to appreciate longer term. And in doing so it will be worth more and more as the network value of Bitcoin increases, and so does its purchasing power.

With more merchants likely to accept Bitcoin in the future, you'll be able to use your Bitcoin much in the same way Hanyecz used his, to buy some pizzas. Albeit for a more reasonable price.

If Laszlo had held on to his, he would have been able to buy a house, a boat, a car, or several of each. That's the aim for you. To be able to use Bitcoin in the future to establish yourself in a position of financial freedom from the constraints of the establishment and the traditional financial authority. To provide you with the ability to secure your wealth in the digital world, to pass on to the next generation, for them to use in the world. To do with however you please.

Remember the core premise of Bitcoin in Nakamoto's white paper?

Online payments to be sent directly from one party to another without going through a financial institution.

It's an anti-financial system. It's revolutionary technology that has the potential to completely change how we think about and manage our finances in the 21st century. And longer term, I think it will have incredibly strong purchasing power.

Which is why I say get some Bitcoin now, with the view to hold it long term and eventually use. In the event that its use isn't as widespread as I anticipate, then there's always the option to sell it back into fiat currency again with the aim of making a profit. Or worst case-scenario, it all goes wrong and you lose your money entirely. That's the outcome if I'm wrong about all this.

But at least you won't die wondering.

I will remind you one more time, this is not your typical financial investment.

Be aware, Bitcoin has no financial backing, no guarantees. It's not regulated by a centralised power like a central bank or government. There may be taxation consequences in different jurisdictions that the world is still trying to figure out. These are all aspects that will apply differently to each individual. You are your own bank and must take on a responsibility for your crypto assets that the current financial system doesn't require of you.

You should also take the time to be sure of any tax and country-specific legal consequences applicable to you.

It's also risky as the comparative fiat value of Bitcoin is volatile for now. As I've said, in the last eight years it's gone from a few cents to over US$19,000 and back again. It's seeing some relative stability now over US$10,000 (at time of writing),, but that might not last. And you could be at risk of losing it all if the price crashes dramatically in a short space of time and you're unable to sell your Bitcoin.

And then if you lose your wallet, don't back it up, have

it stolen, or suffer a cyber-attack, you could also lose all your Bitcoin.

Yes, this has extreme potential in my view. But it also carries its fair share of extreme risk. This journey isn't all going to be smooth sailing. There will be peaks and troughs, highs and lows, but it will be a crazy, fun ride.

This is all part and parcel of Bitcoin – it's a revolution in its earliest stages. And that makes it risky.

It makes the scaling problem a risk. It makes government interference and regulation a risk. It makes all these factors coming together a risk, and pushes people away from Bitcoin and into alternative crypto.

And if you're still in doubt, then think about the value and future potential of Bitcoin like the telephone...

In the early days, when the first telephone was invented, it was of limited value. After all, what can you do with just one telephone? You can't call anyone else. Its value is limited.

But when there were two telephones, you had a network, Albeit a small network. But instantly the value of that telephone network was increased.

And then 10 people had telephones, and again the network was more valuable than before. It had growth potential. As the number of users increased, the value of the network also grew with it.

And in my view it's this "10 users" theoretical position where I think Bitcoin is today. That might sound a little ridiculous, but the reality is not many people really still know about Bitcoin.

Go down to your local high street and look at all the people walking around. Some might have heard of Bitcoin on the news or seen it in the paper. But the number of them currently using it, buying it, sending it, selling it, will be minimal. They don't understand it. They don't get it.

But the same situation existed when the telephone started. It wasn't until people actually got one for themselves that they started to truly appreciate its potential.

And then you had 100,000 people with telephones. Then 1 million. Then hundreds of millions. Then billions. And at that point the network value had increased exponentially.

That's what's going to happen with Bitcoin. As the number of people using it, the number of merchants accepting it, the number of companies building businesses based on it, increases, so will the value of the network, of the blockchain – of Bitcoin.

With widespread, mass adoption one Bitcoin will be worth hundreds of thousands of dollars, millions – as a comparative tool. But the reality is you will be able to buy so much more then with one Bitcoin than you can now. Its purchasing power will rise exponentially with the exponential rise in value of the network.

And the world won't be talking in whole Bitcoin. It will be talking in terms of Satoshi. Remember, Bitcoin might have 21 million Bitcoins in circulation when they're all mined in the year 2140 or thereabouts, but it will really have 2,100,000,000,000,000 (2.1 quadrillion) Satoshi in circulation.

And if one day in the future, in 2140 when all Bitcoins are mined and in circulation – long after you and I have left this world – maybe that coffee from the local coffee store will be just 3 Satoshi. Maybe that Xbox game will cost 45 Satoshi.

Maybe that house you want to buy will cost you 1,000,000 Satoshi.

If that's the situation in the generations to come, then theoretically one Bitcoin (100,000,000 Satoshi) could be the equivalent of US$100 million.

That's the potential I talk about beyond our lifetime when I say that Bitcoin and cryptocurrency today could be the single biggest generational wealth-building opportunity in history that "everyone" has a chance to be a part of.

Bitcoin has the potential to enable any person on earth with enough foresight to get involved, to buy Bitcoin. A chance to mint wealth that you simply would never be able to achieve in the traditional financial system. The system that's rigged towards the already wealthy, the financial elite, the government and their cronies.

But even if those potential futures are still a bit too crazy, a bit too far-fetched, then think about its potential *another* way...

Think about something intangible becoming worth so much that it blows your mind. Think about another similarly intangible object, like a computer operating system.

For example, when you look at Microsoft today it is a company worth US$970 billion. And it makes all sorts of different hardware and software for computers. But when Microsoft began, when Bill Gates and Paul Allen started Microsoft in the 70s, all they did was build an operating system for computers. It was lines of computer code.

And no one, absolutely no one would have been able to predict that in 1974 these two young kids would be starting a US$970 billion company from nothing but computer code.

Consider that today Bitcoin's total network value (the value of all the Bitcoin in circulation) is around US$150 billion. That makes it roughly worth 15% of Microsoft today.

While there's no doubt a company like Microsoft has been important to the advancement of the modern world, the question is, will Bitcoin be more influential? Will it reach and impact the lives of more people?

After all, we're not talking about a company here. We're talking about a completely alternative financial system. Not only do I consider that Bitcoin is more important than any company that exists in the world today, it supersedes the entire financial system.

And if Bitcoin does become more valuable than a simple company like Microsoft, then it would far exceed a value like US$970 billion. But even at that level it would see a 6.5-times appreciation in the current fiat-compared value

– putting it up at over US$55,000.

Again, what would you say if the current fiat-comparative price of Bitcoin were US$8,500? Expensive? Or a bargain?

If you're prepared to accept that, and are prepared to enter the alternative financial system, then I see there being only one direction for you when you consider the future of Bitcoin. And that's to get some for yourself.

Familiarise yourself with Bitcoin further. Set up a Bitcoin wallet. Buy some Bitcoin and transfer into your wallet at the available price at the time. Secure and store your wallet safely. Keep your Bitcoin long term for its potential future purchasing power.

Welcome to the world of Bitcoin and cryptocurrency.

Chapter 15: Ethereum: the next big thing?

Oh wait, did he say Bitcoin and cryptocurrency?

You bet I did. And I've mentioned it a few times already, but there is more than just Bitcoin. I have huge vision for the future of Bitcoin. But there are more cryptocurrencies out there. In fact there are now literally thousands of them.

And one of them has potential to be as big as Bitcoin. Or at least I think it has the potential to be as influential and as valuable as Bitcoin – but the two are explicitly different.

But you must understand these differences, to appreciate its full potential because it isn't like Bitcoin at all.

As I've mentioned a few times now, Bitcoin is really the first crypto "currency" but it's not necessarily the most important crypto that we'll have in the future.

I think that Bitcoin will be the most important and dominant financial instrument, the most common store of wealth as a useable unit of exchange in the future.

But in terms of a crypto that is creating a whole different revolution, you can't look further than Ethereum. Think of this as the better version of the internet – the second internet, the world's computer – the way the internet should have been created in the first place. This is a new social architecture, a new digital infrastructure.

And importantly, Ethereum isn't really a currency, so drop that idea from your mind. This really isn't the "next Bitcoin". It's completely different. It's really not comparative to Bitcoin in its purpose. The real similarity is they both use blockchain technology.

Then again, Ethereum isn't supposed to be a unit of exchange. It's supposed to be a digital infrastructure. It's going to be – and already is – the foundation for a whole new generation of digital assets, digital businesses and digital wealth that's being built on the Ethereum blockchain technology.

But what is Ethereum? What's it all about? What does its future look like?

In the late 80s the World Wide Web (WWW) began to proliferate around the globe. Inventor Sir Tim Berners-Lee had developed a globally interlinked information system that existed on "the internet".

By 1990 a more formal version of the WWW was in development. This resulted in the publishing of the first ever "webpage" on 20 December 1990.

To think that in just 30 years the WWW and internet has gone from obscurity to being almost as important to the world as electricity. I say "almost as important" because without electricity there is no power to make the internet and the WWW work.

The energy source that powers the internet, electricity, is as important to its existence as all the hardware and software that actually makes it work. Electricity is the fuel of the internet – it's vital.

I want you to remember this concept of the "energy" of the internet, as it will help you understand a vital concept about your latest investment recommendation.

The other thing I want you to think about is the opportunity you missed out on. The opportunity you had to invest in the internet and WWW back in the late 80s and early 90s.

Maybe you're one of the smart few that went "all in" investing in the WWW and internet. Maybe you're already a minted multimillionaire. A fortune built on being an early stage-investor in the biggest technological disruption the world has ever seen.

Or, more likely, you're not. That's OK. Most people simply didn't understand the power of the internet at the time. They didn't think that the WWW would take off. No one really could have anticipated things like cloud computing, the Internet of Things or the incredible connectivity that we now have.

It's no exaggeration to say that the internet powers the world. And it's created an untold amount of millionaires and billionaires. If it wasn't for the internet, Mark Zuckerberg couldn't have created Facebook, and he certainly wouldn't be at the helm of a company worth around $520 billion.

You only need to glance down the "20 Youngest Self-Made Billionaires" list in Business Insider to see just how significant the internet has been.

- Evan Spiegel co-founded Snapchat – worth more than $1.8 billion.

- John Collison co-founded online payment company Stripe – worth around $1 billion.

- Nathan Blecharczyk co-founded Airbnb – worth around $3.6 billion.

- Lin Qi founded online gaming company Youzu – worth $1.5 billion.

- Sachin Bansal co-founded Indian online ecommerce company Flipkart – worth $1.4 billion.

These are some of the wealthiest people in the world. And the thing is, they're all under 40 and made their fortune from companies that exist online.

While the internet will continue to mint a whole generation of new millionaires and billionaires (just see the founders of Uber, Lyft, Pinterest, Zoom, etc) it's not the only opportunity in town.

Imagine if you had a second chance at investing in the earliest stage of the internet. Imagine if you could do it with the knowledge that just 27 years later – if you hold steady and ride out the peaks and troughs – you could mint yourself a fortune. Maybe even turn yourself into one of those internet millionaires or billionaires.

Well, this chapter is intended to show you that you have another chance. You have an opportunity right now that's in the same phase the internet was in back in the late 80s and early 90s. It's an opportunity that I believe could turn you *at least* into a millionaire.

That's a grand statement to make. But what if you could turn a $1,000 investment into $60,000 over the next 10 years? That would make you 60 times your money.

Or with another similar investment you could turn $40 into $100,000. That would see you multiply that initial investment 2,500 times – a 249,900% return.

You probably think I'm nuts. A 49,900% return and a 249,900% return in just the next t10 years. Sounds crazy.

But Ethereum is something very special. Something that I think is going to change the world... one of the biggest tech revolutions I've ever seen. And I'll show you how those crazy returns just might be possible.

Ethereum is a global platform that future industry will exist on. I'm convinced it presents you with another huge opportunity for investment – akin to being able to invest in early days of the internet.

You understand Bitcoin and the blockchain by now. How is Ethereum different?

Cryptocurrencies exist exclusively in the online world. And there are hundreds of them. Bitcoin is one, Ethereum is another. Some of the other cryptocurrencies you can buy and sell and trade include Ripple (XRP), Cardano, Stellar, Binance Coin, Zcash, Dash, Tezos and Decentraland.

While I've been researching Bitcoin since 2010, I've also been involved in the world of other altcoins and cryptocurrencies since the beginning of 2013.

After seeing the impact Bitcoin was having on the world I discovered other Bitcoin-like cryptocurrencies that you could buy, use and even sell and trade.

Some of the early altcoins I came across were Libertycoin, Entropycoin, Vericoin, CloakCoin, Mineralscoin, Stealthcoin, Darkcoin, Blackcoin, Counterparty and Ripple.

In fact, in 2015 at the Sibos banking and finance

conference in Singapore, I spoke to the then CEO of the then named Ripple Labs, Chris Larsen, about how their cryptocurrency, Ripple, was going to change the world.

This was before anyone really knew about Ripple and before most people even really knew about crypto at all.

While all of these cryptocurrencies exist solely online, there's something else they typically share. Blockchain technology.

All cryptocurrencies rely on blockchains to function. Many of them work off their own blockchain, which is often based on Bitcoin's blockchain. But there are subtle variations between many of these cryptocurrencies.

One of the more important variations is the difference between what's proof-of-work and proof-of-stake.

Both of these are algorithms that cryptocurrencies can use to create consensus on a blockchain. That means how the blockchain performs its little "audit" and validates transactions against the previous "blocks" that make up the chain.

Achieving consensus allows many different users on the blockchain to agree on the current state and ensure that the next block... and so on... continue to be correct.

Proof-of-work (which Bitcoin employs) uses mining – energy intensive computations – to prove the blocks are correct.

But proof-of-stake uses validators that have a "stake" in the network (a wallet that a person holds a number of coins in) to validate that a block is correct. An example of this I referred to earlier was Tezos (XTZ) where you can earn crypto tokens by simply staking them to help secure the network.

Proof-of-work effectively rewards miners who help power the cryptocurrencies system via the use of hardware and energy inputs. Proof-of-stake can reward stakers, people who retain coins and "lock them up" to help power the system and confirm blocks.

Put simply, one system rewards the energy input to mint coins, the other rewards the commitment input in holding coins.

There is, of course far more complexity to it than this. For example, there are different tweaks developers can make to their proof-of-stake coin to increase or decrease the stake reward for holding coins. We've seen a 140% per annum reward for simply holding and staking coins in a wallet and others around 8%. That smashes the return from most bank accounts and even most dividend-paying shares.

Cryptocurrencies are exciting like Bitcoin because they're decentralised, there's no government control or influence (yet), many of them are anonymous (way more anonymous than Bitcoin) and protect user privacy, and you can transfer them all over the world without delay, interference or exorbitant fees.

But not all cryptocurrencies are "currency". Some of them you should think of as "fuel". They are more like a commodity than a currency. These fuel-like cryptocurrencies have perhaps even a more important role to play in our future digital world. Perhaps they can be more important and *more valuable than Bitcoin.*

And next to Bitcoin, the most important cryptocurrency that exists right now is Ethereum – and its token (coin) Ether (ETH).

While Bitcoin might be the future alternative finance and payments system, in my view Ethereum is the future of the new internet. And its token Ether is as important as a "fuel" for the future digital world that Ethereum is building the infrastructure for.

Another way to think of Ether is a bit like "digital oil". Oil was the lifeblood of the 20th century. It minted untold wealth as the "fuel" that would power the world.

In my view Ethereum and its Ether coin has that same kind of wealth-creation potential.

Ethereum has the potential to be the foundation of every major new digital – and even physical – application for the next 100 years.

You can think of Bitcoin as the future of money... and Ethereum as the future of the internet, applications and corporations.

Let me explain...

What is Ethereum?

Ethereum is sometimes known as cryptocurrency for enterprise. The developers of Ethereum built a blockchain and system that allows people to build businesses on their blockchain.

Think about a city. Full of skyscrapers with companies and people working away. You can imagine Ethereum as the land and the skyscrapers. Ether is the coin that powers the Ethereum blockchain – it's the same as the electricity that powers the city.

Ethereum originally started in 2013 on the back of a white paper by cryptocurrency researcher, Vitalik Buterin. His primary concept was to build decentralised applications using a new digital protocol.

> *Ethereum does this by building what is essentially the ultimate abstract foundational layer: a blockchain with a built-in Turing-complete programming language, allowing anyone to write smart contracts and decentralized applications where they can create their own arbitrary rules for ownership, transaction formats and state transition functions.*

Again, the simple way to view Ethereum is more as a platform for building applications, businesses, enterprise and even new cryptocurrencies. It can achieve this via the use of "smart contracts". These are "autonomous agents" that operate on logic.

For example, if A does B then C does D. These smart contracts can be far more complex than that. They can be as complex as to verify the identity of someone that might be applying for a new trading account. Or they could be a smart contract to pay out a certain amount of money on the delivery of a particular product.

The key point is a smart contract can be used for *anything*. It can be fully automated and trusted. Thanks to the blockchain system and its decentralised nature, it's the perfect tool to build enterprise on.

While I view Ethereum as the world's most important system for future digital business, we also need to make sure we don't dismiss this as just some kind of software platform.

Ethereum is developing in a way where it's almost taking on its own life force. Already there is an entire ecosystem of new applications based on Ethereum.

The best way to get your head around this is to almost think of it like the Apple App Store on the very first day of existence – and then the explosive growth of apps and the billions in wealth it has helped generate.

Investing in Ethereum now is like being on the ground level of day 0 of the app store. This is already creating new enterprise that we never dreamed of existing before.

Take, for instance, an Ethereum-based enterprise called Golem. This is a company that's trying to decentralise computing power. Let's say you've got a nice computer that you regularly use to surf the web. And that's pretty much all you use it for.

It's likely you're using maybe 20% of your computer's processing power. That's 80% you're wasting. But what if you could rent out that 80% or rent to someone who needs more – like a high-end graphic designer. A designer who doesn't want to have to pay the prices for Amazon Web Services or Microsoft Azure. They might not need heaps of computing power all the time. Just some of the time.

So they rent computing power from you, and maybe 10 other Golem users. The renter pays you in Golem. Golem tokens become the method of payment, transfer and fuel for the Golem system of decentralised computer power.

This is a real enterprise. And Golem tokens are real

tradable cryptocurrencies. The thing is, Golem is built and based on Ethereum. Golem might be an up-and-coming digital business, but Ethereum is its core foundation.

The more enterprises develop and build on Ethereum, the more powerful it gets. And I see it developing like the explosion of the internet 25 years ago.

And in order for this Ethereum organism to flourish, in order for the construction of enterprise on Ethereum, it needs energy. It needs fuel. As the Ethereum white paper explains,

> *"Ether" is the main internal crypto-fuel of Ethereum, and is used to pay transaction fees.*

Ether is to Ethereum what electricity is to the internet. And this is an important aspect to understand the future value potential of Ether. Think of it like a commodity. A limited resource that the whole system needs to use to work, but which is in limited supply.

Early investors in Ether will be like the Saudi and Russian oil barons we hear about today. Untold wealth built on holding all the major oil resources from decades earlier.

Imagine in a decade or two being wealthy enough to call yourself an Ether baron. That's the kind of insane potential this just might have.

As Ethereum grows in size and stature, and attracts major global corporations, the value of its fuel, Ether, should rise. And rise... and rise. The bigger it gets, the more it needs Ether. And those that hold it, and use it to help fuel the system could turn into Ether millionaires, maybe even Ether billionaires in the coming future.

What makes me even more confident about Ethereum is that major business is already getting involved.

Early on in Ethereum's journey the Enterprise Ethereum Alliance was formed. This is an "alliance" between giants of the corporate world such as Microsoft, Intel, JP Morgan, BNY Mellon, BP, ING, Thomson Reuters and others.

Its aim is to:

> *Learn from and build upon the only smart contract supporting blockchain currently running in real-world production and to define enterprise-grade software capable of handling the most complex, highly demanding applications at the speed of business.*

This kind of enterprise backing has seen Ethereum become a major alternative cryptocurrency to Bitcoin. ING has even recently undertaken live oil trading on an Ethereum-based blockchain.

According to Coindesk:

> *The live transactions between ING, Société Générale and commodities trading house Mercuria, involved an oil cargo shipment of African crude oil that was sold three times on its way to China.*

And the fuel that powers it all... is Ether.

Today the Ethereum ecosystem is growing at a rapid pace. Everything from fintech to decentralised computing, gaming and gambling, even something as kitsch as collectable kitties exist on Ethereum's blockchain.

I view Bitcoin as a digital, decentralised currency for "the people". Ethereum could well be the supercharged "business version" the world's biggest companies will all come to rely on – the world's computer, decentralised and importantly economically tilted towards users, individuals who create and disseminate data, not a few large siloed organisations.

This is why I think now is the time to get involved in Ethereum and buy Ether. If the growth trajectory of this heads the way I think it will, this could explode in value over the next five to 10 years.

The run has begun... but it's still early days

The good news is that while all this is going on, it's early days yet. Most of these companies are still researching and testing applications on Ethereum. I think it will work, and that major corporations will find use, cost savings and return on investment when they develop Ethereum-based applications.

That's going to push the value of Ether higher. This will also coincide with another major catalyst in the development of the Ethereum system.

Currently the system is based on proof-of-work, like Bitcoin. But the developers of Ethereum are working furiously towards changing that to proof-of-stake.

Doing so would allow Ethereum to increase in scale exponentially, as it would remove the increasingly energy-inefficient reliance on computing power to process the blocks.

Instead proof-of-stake miners become validators and keep the processing requirement under control.

Also, proof-of-stake would put supply constraints on Ether and again push its price.

Proof-of-stake would reward holders of Ether by holding their Ether in wallets to become nodes on the network. In becoming a node and holding (hoarding) Ether, the more Ether you hold, the more important you become in validating the blockchain.

So proof-of-stake incentivises users to hold – not buy and sell – their Ether. This tightens volumes in trading and helps to push the price higher. And don't forget that, as more transactions take place on the system, more smart contracts are built and put in operation. And Ether becomes more valuable to power the system.

Early 2016 the co-founder of Coinbase, one of the most well-funded Bitcoin start-ups ever, suggested that Ethereum could even, "blow past Bitcoin entirely".

He wrote:

> There is nothing that Bitcoin can do which Ethereum can't. While Ethereum is less battle tested, it is moving

faster, has better leadership and has more developer mindshare. First mover advantage is challenging to overcome, but at current pace, it's conceivable.

Imagine if Ethereum could indeed blow past Bitcoin. If you invested in Ethereum now and it went to the price of Bitcoin today, you would turn US$250 into US$8,500. You'd make 34 times your money.

That would turn a $1,000 investment into Ether into $34,000.

But I have much bigger price aims for Ether.

I've been keeping an eye on Ethereum since 2016. And the price of one Ether has already started to accelerate. One Ether is now around US$250.

When Ethereum first launched and was raising money in an ICO, the value was US$1 per Ether. At US$250 per Ether today... well you can see the money some people have *already made.*

But it's not too late. I believe Ether is only just getting warmed up. You can look back and think, oh we wish we'd invested at $1. But you didn't know about it then, so rather than look back... look forward.

The potential of Ethereum and the value of Ether is huge. Maybe even bigger than Bitcoin.

And some major tech players think Bitcoin could go to $500,000. The first investor in Snap Inc. [NASDAQ:SNAP] (Snapchat), Jeremy Liew, said by 2030 Bitcoin could realistically go to US$500,000 per BTC.

He says:

> *Bitcoin's 2030 price and user count total $500,000 and 400 million, respectively. The price is found by taking the $10 trillion market cap and dividing it by the fixed supply of 20 million Bitcoin.*

That would be compelling if you own Bitcoin. But imagine if the same can be said for Ether. If the value of one Ether was still just 0.03 Bitcoin (what it is at the approximate time of writing), that would be US$15,000. Then you'd be looking at 60 times your money from today.

And if Bitcoin hits $1 million in the future – or even if Ether becomes stronger comparative to Bitcoin's price – then the sky is the limit.

This is as early stage as it gets for this kind of breakthrough technology. There's a long road ahead for mass adoption, awareness, usability, understanding and growth.

Both Bitcoin and Ethereum have their place. But I think the potential upside for Ethereum and its token, Ether, is extraordinary. Also, as Ether is mainly exchangeable to Bitcoin, the idea with Ether long term is that you do exit a position and convert back to Bitcoin as your primary way of then using your Ether profits in the real world.

Ether isn't designed to be spent. Bitcoin is. So you must make sure you keep that in mind at all times.

Before you do get involved, though, I strongly recommend reading up more information on Ethereum on its official Ethereum project website, ethereum.org.

How to buy Ethereum?

Like Bitcoin, the next big question I get is obviously, how do I buy Ether?

Over the last three years buying and investing in cryptocurrencies has become significantly easier.

With Ethereum it's very simple to get things started. In many cases now you simply go to a site just like you do with Bitcoin such as Coinbase or Bittylicious, or CEX.io or any other crypto exchange, and simply buy Ether with your fiat money.

But of course by now you might already have Bitcoin. And if that's the case, then great. You're already in the crypto economy. There's another way to get Ether, and that's to exchange your Bitcoin for it, keeping everything within the crypto world.

If you want to trade Bitcoin for Ether then again, you will need to set up an account with a cryptocurrency exchange site. The ones we've used before, include Binance, KuCoin, Poloniex and Bittrex.

While you can trade Bitcoin for Ether, you'll also see you can trade for a whole range of cryptocurrencies.

But the focus here is Ether. Daily volumes of Ether are often in the tens of thousands of Bitcoin per day. Sometimes they can push as high and higher than 100,000 Bitcoins worth of Ether. That means you'll easily be able to get some.

Now you do need to get your Bitcoin into these exchanges to trade Bitcoin for Ether. And that's as simple as sending Bitcoin from your wallet into your exchange wallet.

Don't forget you need the "deposit" address from your exchange wallet 100% correct when sending in your Bitcoin. But once your exchange wallet is loaded, away you go. You're ready to buy Ether.

Go to the "BTC/ETH" market, scroll down to "BUY ETH" and put your order in. It's just like buying stocks – but buying crypto instead. When your order is processed you'll find you'll have Ether in your "Deposits & Withdrawals" tab from earlier.

And much like Bitcoin, you need to withdraw your Ether to your Ethereum wallet. That obviously means you need to install an Ethereum wallet.

This is just like installing a Bitcoin wallet. Remember when I said if you can do it with Bitcoin you can do it with any crypto? Well, this is the proof.

And like Bitcoin, you can use one on your desktop or mobile.

However, as this is a long-term play I recommend using an offline storage device to store your Ether. I use a device exactly like I explained in how to store your Bitcoin – the Ledger Nano S Wallet or a Trezor hardware wallet.

This will allow you to set up an Ethereum wallet and then

also store your Ether on the device offline – protecting against the risk of cyber theft of your Ether.

When you've set up your wallet you will need to copy the address of your wallet and process the withdrawal on your exchange. After a short period of time your Ether should appear in your wallet.

You now own Ether, and have it safely secured and stored.

This might seem a little daunting, but it's not too hard if you've bought some Bitcoin already. Again, if you're still a little unsure, then I recommend starting with small amounts to get used to it before ramping up to buy larger amounts.

Of course, just like Bitcoin, you want to make sure you understand this could all go wrong! Ethereum is still so early stage and full of potential risks, much in the same way that Bitcoin is, that any money you do put into it could all disappear in an instant.

Do not confuse investing in cryptocurrencies with stock-markets or fiat currency markets. While similar in operation to Bitcoin, both are incredibly high risk.

I can't stress highly enough that you are at a serious risk of losing your investment. That means you shouldn't pump your life savings into any of this. Small capital amounts can provide huge upside potential long term – that's what you're looking at.

If it all goes wrong and you do lose your dough, don't say I didn't warn you. This is high-risk investing at the earliest of early stages for future technologies and their huge upside potential.

Like the early days of the internet, it's a bit like the Wild West. There is potential for huge success. There is also potential for complete failure. I've seen cryptocurrencies fail first hand. It's not pretty.

Ethereum, while already establishing itself as a major blockchain provider and developer of cryptocurrency, is vulnerable to failure. Ether could crash in price. Ethereum may suffer a cyber-attack or go through a hard fork, splitting the currency into two streams.

This has actually happened once prior in its early development. Which is why there are two forks of Ethereum. These are Ethereum and the other is Ethereum Classic.

It's important to understand I'm talking here about Ethereum, not Ethereum Classic. While the two share the same history, they are now separate crypto assets.

And this kind of hard fork that split them could happen again. Although the developer team of Ethereum is far more advanced with the project now than it was prior. But a hard fork can happen again, and it's a risk you need to accept.

There's also the risk that other cryptocurrency networks like Ethereum – but better – could appear in the future. These could provide even more compelling opportunities for development and investment.

After all, Bitcoin was the first back in 2009, and Ethereum didn't even exist. Thanks to Bitcoin we now have Ethereum. It's viable to think that, thanks to Ethereum, we will have another major cryptocurrency project, which may be better again.

We've already seen other "layer one" blockchain projects launch since Ethereum's original deployment, such as Tezos, Cardano, Binance Chain, Tron, EOS and others.

Which will succeed? Maybe all of them, maybe just a handful. But in our view Ethereum will continue to be one of the most important and dominant, particularly if it deploys the blockchain with a proof-of-stake consensus mechanism.

I≠ can't know for sure which blockchain will or won't survive into the future so be aware even though Ethereum is dominant now, it's also a risk that you should be aware of that it might not be in the future.

This is high-tech development in the "digital Wild West". Competition risk and technology risk are incredibly high. But the advantage Ethereum has is it's a first-mover with smart contracts and it's already got a huge head start on any potential competitor.

You need to make sure you're ready for everything that Ethereum will throw at you. It's an unregulated market, prone to cyber theft and scams. If you send your Ether to the wrong account or don't properly secure your wallet, you could lose your investment and have little chance of recovering it... ever. That's why I'm a big fan of the offline storage using the Ledger wallet.

While I forecast that Ether has the potential to rise incredibly in price, as high as $100,000, there is no guarantee. The opposite could happen. With incredible upside potential comes incredible risk. It's also volatile, going from $1 just a couple years back to $360. It even went from around $35 to $400 in the space of a few weeks in 2017 and in late 2017 it even topped US$1,000. Another 1,000% increase from previous highs is possible long term – after all, if it can become the new world's computer, internet v2.0, then maybe those aren't all-that-wild predictions.

If you're prepared to accept all the traps and trimmings that come with Ethereum, then come on board. Buy some Ether along with your Bitcoin, and own the fuel of the digital future.

Chapter 16: The ICO effect

For all the importance we associate with Bitcoin and Ethereum there's another crucial piece of the puzzle that you need to understand. These are simply the beginning.

Cryptocurrencies are the new kid on the global financial block. But even beyond global finance there are cryptocurrencies that are redefining everything from how companies raise capital to what the very concept of "money" is to society.

In fact, it's inaccurate to define them all into the one basket of cryptocurrency.

The reality is that many of them don't act like currencies in the traditional sense at all. I've demonstrated that with Ethereum. Its token, Ether, is more like an energy source that powers the Ethereum smart contracts, which operate on the Ethereum blockchain. And at its core Ethereum has become one of the most influential networks of the modern era.

You must view Ethereum as a piece of infrastructure. In fact, you should look at it much the same as you look at the internet.

Now, if you think of the internet, think about all the wonderful companies that we now have thanks to it. As mentioned in the previous chapter, companies like Snap Inc., Facebook, Amazon, these are all only possible because of the mass adoption and widespread release of the internet.

Companies like Apple only experience growth, huge revenues and profits like they do because their phones, computers and tablets are much more than devices you simply call someone on, write a letter on or play *Fruit Ninja* on.

Without the power of connectivity, without the power of the internet, many of these companies would simply be worthless. Can you imagine online shopping with Amazon if the internet didn't exist?

Of course not. Amazon wouldn't exist. There would be no such thing as Amazon Web Services. Without the internet, Amazon is a jungle in South America, as it was before the internet.

So think of Ethereum like the internet.

But think of other cryptocurrencies built on Ethereum like the Amazons, Apples and Facebooks of the new "cryptoconomy".

Crypto like Siacoin, Decentraland, Steem, BAT, Power Ledger, Enigma... these are all new decentralised organisations that are running on the Ethereum blockchain.

However, there are a number of other new crypto projects that are springing up every single day that are using Ethereum's smart contract to perform ICOs.

And this is where the crypto world begins to get really exciting... and dangerous.

Anyone with a bit of programming knowledge can effectively start up their own crypto and launch an ICO. There is no oversight, no regulation, no controls, no way for the average punter to see through the spin and out the other side.

That means someone like you could effectively launch a new company called "MyCoin" put together a well-written white paper, which is basically just a business plan, tool up a nice, HTML5-rich website with all the bells and whistles, set up a Twitter account with lots of hashtags, retweets and paid-for bot followers, and then launch an ICO.

In that ICO you might value your MyCoin token (MCT) at 2,000 MCT per 1 Ether. So if someone wanted to invest 10 Ether (about $2,500) into your ICO they'd get 20,000 MCT. That would place a value of 12.5 cents for 1 MCT.

Here's where it gets oh so easy to sniff out a scam. You could decide to mint 200,000,000 MCT. So if all MCT were minted and in circulation and the value stayed at 12.5 cents, your MyCoin project would have an effective enterprise value of $25 million.

Overnight you could create a $25 million company out of thin air with little more than an idea and some good marketing.

That's the dangerous and exciting part of these ICOs.

There are already companies like Gnosis, TokenCard and Humaniq that did ICOs and raised millions of dollars in ICOs in a matter of *minutes*.

The TokenCard ICO raised over $16.7 million in under 10 minutes. But shortly thereafter it came to light that a "bug" in the ICO meant that some investors who bought Tokencard's "Tokens" using the cryptocurrency "Singles" were able to obtain far more than they should have.

In one instance, a bulk buyer spent $432,000 purchasing 6.2 million Tokens of the 42.3 million total supply. In one swift action one investor controlled 15% of the total stake. So much for decentralised...

Then more recently the Status ICO actually clogged up the Ethereum blockchain so badly that you could barely transact in Ether. This is a big problem, and now a scaling problem that Ethereum faces too.

These ICOs have become a craze of hype, hysteria and FOMO all in their own right. Stupid money being blindly thrown at ICOs hoping to be the next Bitcoin.

I've personally watched a crypto come from obscurity to suddenly be trading in excess of 10,000 Bitcoins worth of volume in a day. It went up more than 500% in a day and then in the space of 20 minutes halved in price.

This is effectively what is known as "pump and dump". And it's much the same as how some penny stocks on markets used to trade. I say "used to" because stockmarkets have far more regulatory oversight than they used to.

But the crypto market has no oversight.

As I said it's the Wild West of the new economy. And I we make pains to explain how volatile, how risky and dangerous this all is, the simple fact is it's early stage. And there's money to be made both in trading these cryptocurrencies, and investing in the right kinds of ICOs that might actually go on to be the next Amazon or Facebook of the crypto world.

But the other reality is the ICO market is a bubble that will pop. And it will clear out the rubbish and leave only the strong to continue. And it's the strong cryptos, the ones with real-world application and network value, like Ethereum, Bitcoin and a select few others, that will live on stronger and more successful once the ICO mania explodes in people's faces.

Now this sentence above came to fruition during the ICO mania of 2017 and 2018.

While some of the tokens mentioned above were early ICO successes, we saw even more and even bigger ICOs late in 2017 as the crypto markets took off in terms of relative fiat-converted value.

Filecoin's ICO, one of the biggest, brought in more than US$250 million in a matter of weeks.

The EOS ICO (or token sale) lasted a year and brought in billions of contributions from investors looking to tap the ICO markets.

We saw projects double in a day, triple in a few days, 10x in a couple of weeks driven by mass hysteria, immense speculation and all-out FOMO.

However, the space quickly became toxic and when a crypto wasn't "mooning", communities were quick to turn against projects. Some projects were outright scams or multi-level-marketing schemes, or worse, Ponzi schemes.

Examples of the dangers of this ICO mania and the fragrant flaunting of laws can be seen by the collapse and pursuit of projects like BitConnect and OneCoin.

BitConnect in particular rose from an ICO price of around 17 cents to $463 by December 2017 – more than a 272,000% gain. But BitConnect was always suspected to be a Ponzi scheme. Still those kinds of gains saw investors blindly tipping into the project.

However, about a month later it shut down, overnight sending the values plummeting and locking up investors BCC tokens, rendering them worthless.

One of the most astonishing statistics that illustrates the ICO boom was the funding that found its way month on month into ICOs.

At the start of 2016 there was virtually no investment into ICOs – they really weren't something of note and around this time the values of crypto like Bitcoin hadn't gone parabolic and really hit the mainstream in a big way yet.

By late 2016 the ICO effect was starting to take shape and September 2016 saw around $20 million of funds flow into various ICOs.

January 2017 saw this figure push higher to around $47 million for the month. But it wasn't until April 2017 when things started to get a little crazy.

The boom in ICO funding coincides with the run in Bitcoin prices, and by May 2017 as Bitcoin's price had gone from US$1,000 to over US$2,000, we saw ICO funding spike to around $228 million.

In June that ICO funding figure spiked again to over US$645 million. Then the following months saw the following ICO funding flows (all figures in USD):

July 2017 – $741 million

August 2017 – $538 million

September 2017 – $988 million

October 2017 – $1.21 billion

November 2017 – $1.54 billion

December 2017 – $2.28 billion

January 2018 – $3.07 billion

February 2018 – $3.01 billion

March 2018 – $2.78 billion

However, soon after February 2018 fiat-converted prices of all cryptos started crashing.

Quickly the ICO effect was over, and values began to plummet as investors that piled into these opportunities rapidly piled out. It was purely reminiscent of the dot-com bubble boom and bust and it was replicating almost perfectly here in ICOs.

By August 2018 ICO funding had dried up to $326 million. By the end of 2018 ICO funding had all but ground to a complete halt, back to early 2016 levels. This saw projects laying off staff, slimlining operations, losing millions in value on crypto contributions, and many just completely shutting up shop and leaving the project in the dust.

It also saw an immense amount of scams, fraud and fakery perpetuate and burn hundreds of thousands, maybe millions of investors in ICOs around the world.

The mainstream media got hold of these collapses and helped to perpetuate the story that the crypto bubble had burst, it was all over and finally (to them) this fake internet money was truly being seen for what it was.

The ICO event of 2017 and 2018 left a bad taste in investors' mouths, left a lasting legacy on mainstream views of crypto markets and lost a lot of people a lot of money.

It was a horrible year – and ended up with many dubbing the aftermath, the "crypto winter".

When we look back through the major events of crypto existence and we talk about the Bitcoin genesis block, 2013's bull run off the back of political instability, we will also always look upon the ICO mania of 2017 and 2018 as a period which we should learn from and understand that it's not good for the healthy development of an ecosystem...

That is, unless the ICO event actually ended up doing more

good for the future of crypto than bad as most would have you believe.

You see, yes, the ICO bubble needed to pop. And a mass clean-up of the crypto ecosystem was and will always be needed-such is the free, unsupervised nature of it all. But what a lot of people forget that only came to the crypto space in 2017, is that the ICO event wasn't the first, maybe won't be the last and in fact, has resulted in a crypto winter if you only look at fiat prices... but has really resulted in one of the most promising periods in crypto history, the Buidl Era.

Chapter 17: the Buidl Era

"Crypto winter is here."

That was the overwhelming response to the bust of crypto prices during 2018. We had seen Bitcoin's fiat-converted price exponentially rise during 2017 and then not even a few months later in early to mid-2018 prices were collapsing.

I've seen this pattern several times before in Bitcoin and other crypto. In fact, Bitcoin's trajectory over time is littered with examples of massive exponential runs higher, "crashes" then returns to higher highs from there. These secondary and third movements higher make the previous "bubbles" look like nothing more than a blip on the charts.

Each time, however the masses are quick to forget we've been here before and that each time brings a number of critical elements of the Bitcoin and wider crypto ecosystem.

One such benefit of these boom and bust cycles is awareness. It's not necessarily the way you want to get awareness, but it's there nonetheless. Sometimes bad press is good press... isn't that what "they" say?

Another benefit is capital. Bitcoin value increases mean there's capital to flow around to dedicate to development and progress. But that only comes when the third element is present, and each cycle, the bigger it gets, brings human capital to the ecosystem. And in the latest crypto winter it's this deployment of human capital that's been so crucial to the crypto world never being as strong as it is right now.

I can say this because I've seen this space grow over the last nine years, and in the last few years while prices have been volatile, there's never been as much progress, growth, development and innovation. In fact, I'd say I've never seen any industry in history show such promise with what they're able to buidl in such a short space of time facing such opposing headwinds.

The crypto community is something else, and they can buidl better than anyone out there.

I explained earlier in Part 1 the events that shaped Bitcoin and crypto forever and about the terms "hodl" and "Buidl". As you now understand, buidl comes to signify that the community, developers, the builders of crypto projects, blockchains, code, applications, are all furiously working away on not just crypto, but ways in which we can use decentralised networks and applications with this new technology, to change the world.

But of course it comes in waves, and this era of buidl did come at a cost to many investors as I said earlier, having possibly been burnt for life about coming near crypto again. But you've got to consider that long term, this could be exactly the place you need to be involved in, through the good and the bad times, to really appreciate, understand and reap the full rewards of the potential that's on offer.

I know what the feeling is like to see your crypto portfolio be worth huge amounts of fiat-converted money, and just months later, fractions of that previous value.

It really hurts. It makes you question why you bother with this "toy money" anyway? It makes you think you'd have been better off jamming your cash under the bed and filling in online surveys all year instead.

I know that feeling because I've been there, three... four times now, or is it five? To be honest we I count after the third crypto boom and bust cycle.

And there's a bloody good chance in the years and decades to come as you continue your crypto investing, you'll see another of these again too.

But what we've historically seen, at least in crypto, is that the next time around things reach higher highs, making the previous vicious cycle look like a blip on the radar. Now, of course, we can't guarantee that's going to happen again this time around.

However, there is something that gives us the confidence to say that if you can survive these so-called crypto winter events, you'll come out the other end shining.

And that is the entire crypto space, Bitcoin, Ethereum and altcoins (in general) are in a better position than they were before the boom and bust cycle and significantly better than they were at the peaks of these price rises.

Every time we go through this, things get better.

Crypto is in a better position than it was two years ago. They're in a better position than they were in 2013 during the first altcoin hype cycle.

That's the thing when you appreciate this is a *technology revolution* and not a speculative bubble.

This is more akin to the development and proliferation of the internet – and you quickly realise it cannot be stopped. It only gets better.

The critics say there's nothing tangible there, nothing backing any of it, but Microsoft was just software to start with. Uber doesn't own any cars but merely derives massive value from its global network.

The World Wide Web isn't a "thing" but it was the catalyst for arguably to date the biggest wealth-creation event in history.

Remember the potential crypto and blockchain technologies have to disrupt industry all over the world. This is a mega-trend the likes of which we see maybe once every half century or so. It's a wealth-creation opportunity that could change lives. And it's at such an early stage that it's difficult to be a part of with the levels of risk and volatility that are involved.

2018 and into 2019 and the crypto winter that so many were bemoaning, in my view, had all the hallmarks of the periods of development and ultimately recovery we've seen from previous boom and bust cycles in crypto.

But how do I know that things are being built, development is taking place and the important conversations and considerations are taking place?

I fortunately get to exist on the inside of this world and get to visit, listen to, see, speak with and question the people who are building all the elements of the global crypto infrastructure and ecosystem.

I've seen those from projects like Binance, Coinbase, Zilliqa, Tendermint, Elixxir, OKCoin, Kyber, Ethfinex, Bithumb, MyEtherWallet, blockchain.io, IOTA, Ripple and Bitcoin. I've seen the view and vision for regulatory bodies like the EU Commission, the SEC, CBOE, Australian Securities and Investments Commission, Financial Conduct Authority and other global regulators.

And importantly, we understand at this juncture in crypto where the next big money flow is coming from. As the previous chapter outlines, the ICO market is all but dried up, but that doesn't mean massive money isn't coming to crypto.

Traditionally in finance you find that institutional money, endowment money, private family office money, flows into the big opportunities before retail investors get a chance to even think about it. That means the bulk of opportunity and life-changing gains goes to those who are already rich.

Ask yourself, did you get a chance to seed Facebook, Uber or Amazon in the early days? What opportunities did you have to generate real wealth from the internet and app economy before these got to a public market well after the real money was made?

But in crypto this script is flipped on its head. And this time it's the average person, the retail investor with a bit of foresight that has the jump on the big money of the world. And that's a major shift in power across global finance, as it changes the rules of the game and gives everyone a real chance at wealth.

When I say the big money is only just coming to crypto, here's a good example of things. At the 2019 Paris Blockchain Week I was able to listen to the comments of the CEO and co-founder of Morgan Creek Capital Management, Mark Yusko.

The panel session was called "State of the Art: Institutional Investments in the Crypto Space". And on the panel was Yusko, Charlie Meraud (Woorton), David Fauchier (Cambrial) and Andrew Robinson (Coinbase).

The discussion was excellent. And they all agreed that institutional money, big pension funds and endowment funds were not invested in this crypto space... yet. But that money is primed and ready to come once the right metrics are in place for them to get involved.

But what Yusko was saying is that some are already dipping in via funds like Morgan Creek that then go on to invest in this space for them. Yusko noted that Morgan Creek was raising its second fund for US$250 million investing in the crypto space. And that up until early 2019, Morgan Creek hadn't bought crypto directly...

That's when it *started* buying Bitcoin. And as Yusko put it, "doubling down" on the crypto space. In particular, he likened what's happening to the great technology revolutions of our time, from the development of the microprocessor, the personal computer, the internet and the mobile revolution.

This is an important point to make. This long view on crypto and Bitcoin isn't just me. I'm no evangelist. I'm a technologist and futurist at heart, I look for life-changing tech trends and investigate and research them to their fullest. But in doing that, as part of my life's work, I was lucky enough to get involved in crypto early on because it's a technology revolution, and it had all the hallmarks of a world-changing mega-trend that could change *everything*.

Yusko went on to explain the next step in the evolution of global networks, decentralised connectivity and crypto as "TrustNet" and believes that it will surpass every one of those massive technology events that's come before. He put a window on it to 2024. And he noted that he believes it will be the greatest wealth-creation event the world has ever seen.

That's a view we both share.

The crypto winter is really perfect for the long-term explosion of wealth that's up for grabs. Right now, the crypto ecosystem has never been healthier, never been as thriving as it is now.

And that's building up to a massive change in how society interacts, communicates and transacts with each other. And it's those of you now that are in this space, investing in this space that will be looked back on as pioneers.

It's all still early stage, and there's a huge swathe of the masses and markets and money that's not yet even dipped their toe into the crypto space. But it's coming. And it's going to bring immense opportunity when it does.

It also means there's going to be opportunity galore, in quality, long-term, viable investment plays over the coming years. It's not all about the short term, but what kind of portfolio can you build over the next few years to be entrenched in a world where we're talking about digital assets like cryptocurrency, crypto-stocks, crypto-commodities, crypto-bonds, crypto-assets.

These are the kinds of developments in the buidl era that are coming. Did you ever think you'd be able to undertake a contract of sale for a car using blockchain technology to instantly transfer all ownership rights and make payments to the seller instantly?

What about buying a house where all title deeds and, again, contracts are executed at the time a sale is agreed? We're talking about processes that traditionally took weeks, maybe months and great expense, being done instantly and with virtually no cost.

Or when you look at the global payments and remittance markets, someone that might be working in the US for example but remitting money back to Indonesia would have to use middlemen and intermediaries like Union Pay, Western Union or retail banks to send money from one country to another.

It comes at great cost with exchange rate spreads, commission costs and transaction costs on both ends. These fees tally up into the double digits often. That money is crucial to the existence and way of life of billions of people. Yet along the way it's clipped off by a system designed to profit the few, take from the many, and make the already elite and rich, more elite and rich.

But today you can send cryptocurrency from one place to anywhere else on earth instantly and at almost no cost. I once remember sending a few ETH tokens to my brother from the UK to Australia. It took less than a minute and cost no more than 2 cents.

This kind of capacity never existed before crypto. It has changed the game and will continue to do so.

But then during this period we're now also seeing globally massive organisations now get interested and involved in crypto in a way they've never been able to or interested in doing before.

Again, the critics will say, "Blockchain has no use cases." They doubt it and chastise it because they haven't seen it in action. And because they can't see the future... or past the end of their noses.

They are blind to the progress that I see on a near daily basis. Or perhaps they just have loftier expectations for a technology – that is barely 10 years old – trying to dethrone an entrenched system that is almost as old as civilisation itself.

In the long run we'll see who has the last laugh. It's pretty clear to me that the writing is on the wall anyway.

I'm not alone in my thinking either. IBM has already debuted its much-talked about World Wire project. This is a global payments system that is built upon the Stellar [XLM] protocol, which is made possible by Stellar's blockchain.

Not only is it a giant middle finger to the blockchain sceptics, it is also a huge step towards improving our messy and outdated global payments systems.

The current, convoluted system of payments is a hodgepodge of back and forth transfers and settlements. And each step of the way naturally takes a cut of the overall transaction.

It's imperfect, but it's the only means people have had to mobilise their money around the world. At least until now.

IBM's World Wire, aims to streamline this process. As it states, it will be "the first blockchain-based network that integrates payment messaging, clearing, and settlement on a single network."

That's an impressive feat, and we hope it can live up to the hype. Not just to prove the blockchain critics wrong, but to provide a modern solution to our global financial needs.

Now these are all huge steps forward, but it's important to know that in the Buidl Era, we also have to be careful not to buidl these great systems but neglect the fact that at the end of the day this should be life-changing and accessible to the masses, to everyone... and that means achieving a critical moment we all need to be on the lookout for. It's the tipping point when we know that crypto is all set to properly boom again.

This next massive leg-up, is going to be determined by a particular sub-set of our population. And if you've still got one lying around somewhere, you can use them to test out the next massive crypto wave.

I call it the "Nan Moment".

Sadly, all my grandparents have since moved on to another part of the multiverse.

But now I've got a kid, that suddenly makes my dad, my

wife's mum and dad, automatic "nans and pas". So that's helpful, as I can use them to test my thesis.

It's a simple premise really, if your nan (or pa) can use a dApp (decentralised application) built on a crypto blockchain, then it's easy enough for everyone. And if it's easy enough for everyone, then real-world usage of crypto networks is going to explode.

In short, we should all be regularly testing out crypto applications and platforms using nans and pas as our test subject. Think of it as a non-harmful clinical trial... for crypto.

We're close but we're not there yet. But in the Buidl Era I think we'll get there. Here's a few more examples of what we've seen come to the fore in the current Buidl Era.

I dove into tipping on Twitter using Bitcoin. That means sending a micropayment to someone for something that you saw and liked on Twitter.

There was a browser extension, tippin.me, which I installed to make micropayment tips through Twitter. Now on the face of it this seemed easy, like it was going to pass the nan test (a nan with Twitter that is).

Anyway setting up the browser extension was easy enough... but then it got a little complicated.

I had to set up a Bitcoin Lightning Channel on the Lightning Network in order to make and receive tips. You see while the tips are Bitcoin, it's facilitated through the Lightning Network.

Well there's a roadblock for nan off the bat. Nan isn't going to want to go and deal with something that's not called Bitcoin. Game over.

The further detail for me meant I had to find a wallet to open the Lightning Channel. But then I had to fund the Lightning Channel with Bitcoin. Why? Well, with Lightning, you fund the channel you need to open with another party and that's the amount it can send and receive. You can do unlimited instant transactions between the parties up to the value of the channel. Then when you close the channel, the actual BTC is distributed out.

Sound complex? That's because it is. Again this is all important technical information and requirements, but it's irrelevant to the end user.

Nan just wants to pick something up and use it, not have to establish all these things before just making a simple Bitcoin tip.

While the benefit of the Lightning Network is huge for Bitcoin, it's still too complex. And the upside of instant and insanely cheap BTC transactions is great. But it's not a great user experience... for now. In terms of the nan test, the Lightning Network would fail dismally.

But there are developments coming where soon enough it may pass the nan test with flying colours. I know there's development work going into an internet, "web protocol" called WebLN, which could become a Bitcoin Lightning Network payments standard across the internet.

In that sense it would be as simple as a point and click to send BTC payments across the internet. An example provided by the developer, William O'Beirne, as reported by Coindesk:

> "[Think about a] *WebLN-enabled site that allowed users to quickly paying a Satoshi (worth about $0.00004) to get rid of advertisements for the day*."

I think that day is coming fast at us when Bitcoin will be "the internet's currency". Where you can use Bitcoin as a fast, easy, flexible way to make and receive payments through the digital world.

Think about instant BTC micropayments for YouTube or another content platform, or to get rid of ads for the day, or to read an article behind a paywall. No need to compromise your security and privacy by entering credit card details and address details every time you want to pay for something small online. Just tiny fractions of

Bitcoin using the Lightning Network.

But that's the direction of Bitcoin using the Lightning Network, and it's pretty close to passing the nan test.

These are all examples of what happens in crypto during these crypto winter periods. For the outside observer they're cataclysmic events that make crypto a living hell, and it can turn away a lot of people that will ultimately miss out on the big picture opportunity.

But this isn't crypto winter. These periods are opportunities to buidl something great. And right now we're seeing arguably the greatest ever Buidl Era that crypto has ever seen.

It's building something world changing and if you can see it like I do, then I think you're ready to immerse yourself in this opportunity like never before.

Chapter 18: Pushbacks and potential

You only need to look at the list of the most valuable cryptocurrency to see there's a real ecosystem building here. Just three years ago, back in mid-2014, the biggest cryptocurrency was Bitcoin. It had a market cap then of around $8 billion.

Litecoin was another of the biggest. It had a market cap around $300 million. Even Dogecoin, which started as a joke coin (seriously), had a market cap of $35 million. Ethereum, Cardano, Tron and Tezos didn't even exist. Even Dash was only just starting out.

Today Bitcoin's market cap is north of $150 billion. Ethereum, which only launched its ICO in 2015, has a circulating supply worth $29 billion. Binance Coin, worth $4.7 billion, Stellar $2.6 billion. Tezos, just a couple years old, has a circulating supply over $1 billion. And Dash has gone from a market cap of around $750,000 in 2014 to $1.4 billion in 2019.

Many of the "long termer" coins that were around in 2014 and have survived this long have seen their value increase 100-fold and more. Imagine being an early investor in Dash for example, back in 2014. $1,000 worth of Dash back then would be worth almost $1.76 million today. That's the kind of return that early Bitcoin investors were making.

And that's what makes the world of crypto so very exciting. There are opportunities like Bitcoin, Dash, Tezos, Binance Coin and Ethereum to make money that you simply would never make in any other market in the world.

And most mainstream people still have absolutely no idea there's money to be made or how to go about making it. Most people I talk to are still afraid about buying Bitcoin. They see it as worthless because it isn't backed by anything physical. Yet somehow they believe the money that sits in their online bank account with their "trusted" bank is more than 0s and 1s. They think that money has some kind of "backing".

But frankly they just don't know how the current system works nor are they getting the right information about the potential of what the cryptoconomy can do for them.

Now much of this is a problem about the potential versus the pushback.

You see for all the potential of Bitcoin and crypto, there's a huge pushback from traditional investment, government, regulators and mainstream media about this burgeoning ecosystem.

They see it for all the wrong reasons and not many of the good ones. There are a few beacons of light amongst the pushback, but right now it's a very adversarial approach to things.

It's more about how can we control crypto rather than how can we embrace this technological revolution

As I say, some regions are stepping in with open arms to it all; Malta in particular, France and the UK are taking relatively progressive approaches to blockchain technology and Bitcoin.

But the likes of the US and China are still very much about command and control. But outside of regulators and government, it's apparent that every traditional financial "expert" also has a view on things. Even with astonishingly superficial understandings of what's actually going on in the Buidl Era, they still profess to be experts in this field, because they happen to be financial experts.

Take for instance, comments from Warren Buffett. He's possibly known as the greatest investor of all time. He's a billionaire, has turned around countless companies and has benefited from having large chunks of money to leverage into those opportunities I mentioned before that the average person never gets.

His view on Bitcoin is quite distinct, and uninformed.

Prior to a Berkshire Hathaway annual meeting Buffett said to reporters,

"It's a gambling device... there's been a lot of frauds connected with it. There's been disappearances, so there's a lot lost on it. Bitcoin hasn't produced anything.

"I'll tear off a button here. What I'll have here is a little token...I'll offer it to you for $1000, and I'll see if I can get the price up to $2000 by the end of the day... But the button has one use and it's a very limited use."

This is the kind of pushback and headwinds that Bitcoin and crypto faces... has always faced.

As I've mentioned a couple of times, in 2014 I was on an American TV news show, *The Rick Amato Show*. I was there to talk about Bitcoin in light of the Mt. Gox bankruptcy.

Opposing my views on Bitcoin was a prospective senator for California, Andrew Blount. Both Amato and Blount were highly sceptical of Bitcoin and Blount compared Bitcoin to bubble-gum wrappers. He was adamant Bitcoin wouldn't be around by the end of the year – the interview was in February 2014 – and I explained to them it had far more potential than they were clearly capable of understanding.

I told them it would be around longer than any of us lived. And thus far we can see who's right.

This is what Bitcoin and crypto face every day in trying to get the understanding and message across to the masses about the potential on offer. But it always faces pushback... that is until one day it's so ubiquitous and abundant that people who weren't smart enough to listen and understand, will have missed out on a life-changing opportunity.

Here's a good way to think about what exists in front of you in terms of opportunity...

I remember the first time I saw a mobile phone in person. While I don't remember the exact year, I do remember what it looked like. And I do remember I was still at school. That would roughly put the time frame in the late 80s early 90s.

It was a big chunk of a thing. Far bigger than the handset you'd find on pay phones at the time. But the most notable thing on it was the giant rubber aerial sticking out the top of it. I remember that aerial because I can vaguely remember my brother whipping me on the legs with it, and dad not being happy about playing with it in such a way.

Back then not many people had mobile phones. After all, why would you really need one unless you were a big-swinging business person? If I wanted to call someone, I'd call from the home phone. Or if by chance you needed to call someone when out, you'd use a pay phone, perhaps even with one of those phone cards.

Sometimes they answered, sometimes they didn't. That would then lead to other self-motivated actions like walking home or taking the bus. Or burning some time at the shops and then calling again – and then walking home.

It was an interesting time to be alive. It was also one of those exciting times when you would go on holiday with the family. That's not out of the ordinary you might think...

Except when you went on a holiday in the 80s and 90s no one else knew what it was like until you got home. You'd take the film out of the camera, pop down to the shops – usually the Kodak section at the pharmacy – and get the film developed.

You'd then head over to the food court, grab a muffin and milkshake from Muffin Break, do some grocery shopping at Safeway, then go pick up the pictures. Some of the pictures would have a thumb over them, some would be out of focus or out of framing. And you'd maybe get a dozen or so decent ones that you'd pop into the photo book when you got home.

Ah, the good old days...

I also remember the day we got our first digital telephone. We headed down to Brandon Park Shopping Centre in the South Eastern suburbs of Melbourne, Australia. We parked the car and headed towards the Tandy electronics store.

The phone itself was wireless. Incredible really, because the phone downstairs (an old rotary dial phone), you had to stand next to when talking to someone. But this new one (a Panasonic) you could walk all over the house with it. Incredible stuff.

It wasn't too long after that we got our first flat-screen TV as well. It was a 62cm (because TVs weren't measured in inches yet) Samsung flat screen. The screen was square, I mean, why would it be anything except square? It was a beast of a thing, deeper than it was wide and it took two of us to lift it.

Money also was predominately cash. We had bank cards and you could get money out at the bank teller or ATM. Occasionally you'd use the bank card to pay in the shop, but it was better to just get the cash before you went in.

We paid for that phone and TV in cash.

There's a reason for this trip down memory lane and it's because people often forget how fast things move. But this wasn't more than 20 years ago and in the scheme of things, 20 years is a blip on the radar.

And, more importantly, people forget that technology progress is exponential. The term we prefer to use is technological compounding. It's something we've written about for years now, but it's a simple idea – new technology is built on new technology, creating ever more advanced technology.

It's like how your money would compound with interest, except it's not money, it's technology. What's exciting though is when you can see the obvious trends then you can also make money if you can appreciate the relative nature of time – and have a little patience.

Now, there's a lot of so-called experts out there that say one of the downsides of Bitcoin is it's not suitable as a currency. I beg to differ.

In fact the Bank of International Settlements (BIS) released a survey explaining that:

> *Usage of cryptocurrencies is assessed to be either minimal ('trivial/no use') or concentrated in niche groups.*

According to an article in *Forbes*:

> *The survey revealed that most BIS member central banks think cryptocurrency use "will remain minor" due to "low retail acceptance, compliance issues, better public understanding by the general public of the risks involved and, for some jurisdictions, outright bans."*

The BIS has form when it comes to criticism of Bitcoin and cryptocurrencies. In 2018 it put out a scathing report on the flaws of decentralised systems and cryptocurrencies.

Frankly though, after reading it, we think it's more a "BS" report than a report from the BIS.

It's clear the lengthy 114-page report was put together over a period of time – from my view it seems perhaps work started early 2018 – right at the peak of crypto mania version three. And we all know with the speed of crypto advances and development, the report was already out of date by the time it was released.

In the report, the BIS analyses cryptocurrency, the problems and risks they see. And some of its claims are valid. But you also have to put its perspective... into perspective.

It comes from a background where according to them "central authority" is crucial in the operation of a monetary and payments system. The very idea a decentralised system or a lack or central authority is foreign to the BIS.

It also make the mistakes of speaking about central banks as "trusted". But you also need to ask the question, trusted by whom? And, trusted to do what?

If you're talking about the manipulation of currencies to affect economic "stability", then yes, that's how central banks function. But their track record is pretty poor.

Add to the mix that the purchasing power of a dollar decreases over time and you fast realise that money isn't a store of value in the sense that it should be. Certainly not how the BIS describe it.

What people – like the BIS – need to get their head around is that "money" as we know it is changing.

Working in a financial services business, our compliance department often have to put a big, fat disclaimer into our work. It usually reads:

Past performance is no guarantee of future performance.

And that's true. You shouldn't rely on what something has done in order to figure out what it could do. But where do you see that disclaimer at the central bank? What about the dollars in your pocket, is there a disclaimer on that $20 note?

Your "money" – by that we mean dollars and cents – will be worth less tomorrow than it is today. That's a fact. That's the impact of inflation that the bank "targets" every year.

Now you might not see it on a daily basis, because the number doesn't change. But your money's purchasing power does. And tomorrow it will purchase less.

Now this isn't to say crypto (currencies or assets or whatever) is the perfect solution. But the BIS and other traditional financial system institutions suffer from a bad dose of arrogance.

The current financial system is far from perfect. It's far from "trusted". And perhaps they should consider the fact the world has a money problem. Both how it's created, and how it's abused.

Furthermore, the BIS idea that Bitcoin or the "quest for decentralised trust has quickly become an environmental disaster" is laughable.

Take a stroll down Canary Wharf, London at night time. This is where a lot of the-world's major financial institutions operate.

At night, all those buildings have floors and floors with lights on and computers on. They would have data centres whirring away in the background or remote locations. Their lifts and security systems will be on the go 24/7.

Let's also not forget these institutions exist in billion-dollar buildings that for half the day are unoccupied. I see the same thing when I'm in Melbourne, Sydney, Toronto, Dubai, New York. In fact every major city I go to is like this.

Where's the assessment of the "environmental disaster" the current financial system effects? After all, that's one of the BIS major contentions about the negative impact of Bitcoin. Best not throw stones in a glasshouse we think.

These sorts of pushbacks against crypto are simply fear mongering. They lack depth of research. They lack understanding of the broader ecosystem. They reek of mainstream, superficial analysis carrying an incredible amount of bias.

Now of course as I said, crypto in its current guise isn't a perfect solution... yet. But it's an alternative system trying to fix a broken system. It's trying to build a better way.

Nothing is ever going to be a perfect solution. But at least with crypto you can work towards as close to perfect as you can. And you can do it fast and with the combined knowledge of anyone, anywhere.

The beauty of crypto is that anyone can take part. If you want to contribute to the codebase of a project, most of the time you can. It's because it's open source. If you want to develop your idea on the Ethereum protocol, you can.

But when was the last time you had a chance to contribute to the development of the economy. When could you apply innovation to the cash issued by the central bank?

When was the last time you got to influence the creation of financial products the banks put together? My guess is never.

But through open source, distributed networks you can. Crypto is a technology revolution. And it's more than just finance. It is infrastructure, it is data, it is identity, the monetisation of information, and more.

You can create with it, you can disrupt and effect change with it. You can develop it, work on it and make it better. It's not a stagnant thing. It's evolving, improving, expanding and changing.

Yes, it has issues. And yes, right now it's not the answer we all seek. But when you see the progression and the grunt work of the people working on it, you can see the huge future potential.

The likes of the BIS can write 1,000 reports. It's just their view. And maybe they're right. But I don't believe they are. Not based on what I read in the report by the BIS. I think they simply don't get it. Maybe they never will – maybe they don't want to.

Of course there's always danger that government also wants to get their grubby mitts on crypto. They want to regulate it, control it and have a hand in it.

Remember, one of the core principles of cryptocurrency is its decentralised nature. That means it's free from central bank interference and government control.

This is what makes cryptocurrency so appealing. However, this does not please central banks or governments. Cryptocurrency is a threat to the control of these centralised powers.

And that's exactly why central banks and governments

want a bigger say in how cryptocurrency works.

Jens Weidmann is the president of the Deutsche Bundesbank. And Weidmann doesn't like Bitcoin or cryptocurrency. He thinks it will worsen future financial crises. And he blames its decentralised nature. Weidmann thinks central banks know what's best for everyone. And he doesn't like the thought of currencies outside their control.

For a start, Jens must clearly believe there will be another crisis. The fear of a fresh crisis is one reason why there's already been a flight away from central bank-controlled money and into cryptocurrency. But Weidmann must not have figured that out yet.

He thinks that central banks should issue their own cryptocurrency instead. He thinks it's safer for everyone. In other words Weidmann actually *likes* cryptocurrency – just not ones that he and his cronies in the Bundesbank can't manipulate.

We're pretty sure Weidmann missed the memo that people like cryptocurrency *because* the central bank can't touch it. They like it because government can't influence it. They like it *because it's decentralised.*

It's not just Weidmann who wants to get their grubby mitts on cryptocurrency.

The former Australian Labor Party leader Bill Shorten also had a view on Bitcoin. You see, Shorten thinks that Bitcoin is a safe haven for terrorists. He said in mid-2017,

> *"There are two things we simply do not know enough about to deal with properly–I refer to the use of the digital currency Bitcoin and the use of the dark web, a network of untraceable online activities and hidden websites, allowing those who wish to stay in the shadows to remain hidden."*

This is a ploy for the Australian government to spy on and monitor every citizen and their activities. It loves to use the threat of "terror" to push the thumb down harder on its citizens.

Australia is fast becoming the ultimate nanny state. It's

the modern form of Big Brother – and it's *another* reason why the world is switching to Bitcoin and cryptocurrency.

The government can try and stop it. The central banks can try manipulating it. But it's decentralised. It's out of their reach. It's bigger than government. And it's bigger than the traditional financial system.

But for every day that cryptocurrency gains traction, builds a stronger user base, sees a new ICO, launches another decentralised blockchain, another government comes out in objection to it. Another central banks says it's a worry, perhaps a Ponzi scheme, even the centre of the next major financial crisis.

But they don't get it. They don't see that this is a decentralisation of their power out to people. And therein lies the true revolution in crypto. It's building a new social architecture, a new internet, new funding methods. It's a whole new alternative financial system with the potential to include *everyone*.

The truth is that the global banking system is broken. And it's the new cryptoconomy that's going to change it all.

For now the cryptoconomy is the Wild West, though. There are just as many sharks, con artists and scammers in the crypto world as there are in the real financial world. Yet most people still feel comfortable with their money in the traditional banking system.

But the inherent beauty of cryptocurrencies is the blockchain technology they are all based on. Sure there are subtle differences, different unique offerings, different layers of anonymity, different kinds of applications, wallets, ways in which to use them. But they (mostly) all rely on a blockchain.

And you can't cheat the blockchain. Its decentralised nature makes the system more trustworthy than the global banking system we use today. That's the real gem in all of this. The very system that drove the creation of crypto now wants a piece of the action.

And because of the decentralised nature, scam artists get found out and get weeded from the system. The network, the blockchain, the community operates as one, as a whole, as a trusted system and represents the ultimate free market.

The decentralised, free market that is the cryptoconomy is inherently anti-establishment. It's purely libertarian. It's pure potential that through sheer progress combats all the pushback from the mainstream I see every day.

That's really what I think Satoshi Nakamoto was aiming for when he published the Bitcoin white paper and started all this. He was looking for a way for people to operate independently of the controls of the government. Independently of those who oversee us and think they know what's best for us.

The truth is if you put the power in the hands of the people and a truly free market, then the collective will decide what is best. Blockchain technology, Bitcoin, Ethereum, cryptocurrencies all over the world are proof that the world can adapt, change and develop something truly great. A real once-in-a-lifetime opportunity. With no input from authorities and nefarious influences within government departments.

The crypto world is freedom. And it's just starting. As the years roll by, the market of crypto will develop. It will mature. The high level opportunities that you see with Bitcoin, Ethereum, Dash and others will not be as prevalent. You will see stupid money chasing returns in trashcoins and get-rich-quick schemes.

There is money to be made in crypto and at break-neck speed, but no one ever made a fortune working just five minutes a day from home by following a simple crypto trading strategy. Don't fall for the scammers, know how to identify them and protect yourself not just in the crypto world, but in the financial system you use today.

The ecosystem is evolving and, importantly, there's capital flow coming at a scale that we've never seen the likes of before.

You will see the smart money bunker down into a set few number of cryptos that hold real long-term potential to revolutionise the world's global finance and banking system. Crypto that has the potential to revolutionise the corporate world. To develop a network like the second coming of the internet and see incredible businesses flourish and thrive on these new blockchain networks.

Now and only now is the time to make the kinds of returns and gains as investors that you perhaps would have had back in the 80s. Imagine being the person who invested in Steve Jobs and Steve Wozniak when they were still putting together the first Mac in a garage. Then cashing out a few decades later, when the company they built topped $900 billion.

Now imagine doing that again, but in crypto. And instead of cashing out a few decades later, doing it within one decade. And instead of cashing out, using your crypto to operate in the new financial system.

That's the kind of explosive potential I see the crypto opportunity presenting. You don't often, as an investment professional, see once-in-a-lifetime opportunities to make a play that could redefine your entire career.

But that's what I see here. That's why I think it's the best play into a new market opportunity that's perhaps ever existed. And that's why I'm educating you in all things Bitcoin, Ethereum and cryptocurrency related.

You have to know this market opportunity inside and out. You need to understand Bitcoin, its nuances its origins, the origins of the cryptocurrency world. You need to know why Ethereum is so radically different and why in just two years it has become as important as, if not more important, to everything blockchain and crypto-related than Bitcoin.

And you need to know that other opportunities like these exist now, and will come in the next few years. Opportunities as the cryptoverse matures and presents chances to invest and make money while the mainstream are still napping.

The world of cryptocurrencies, the cryptoconomy, is like nothing else we've seen before. It may not be like anything we'll see for another 30, 40, 50 years... maybe longer.

And once you see, really see, what's happening right under your feet, right at the end of your keyboard, you'll see just how easy this can be. How risky and dangerous it is. How exciting and how wonderful an opportunity this world is to you, to your kids or your future kids, their kids, and generations to come.

The world is going crypto, and right now you've got a chance to be one of the earliest proponents of it. So grab this chance with both hands. Run with it. See the opportunity for what it is, and take a punt on the future.

And if it pays off the way I think it will, then you'll be a crypto convert for life. And maybe even one day people will talk about you as one of the barons of crypto.

This is such an extraordinary change to the very concept of global finance, connected networks, the decentralisation of power, that it's a genuine revolution.

There is a shift of money, and shift of power and shift of social views, behaviours and a shift of ideas and ideals of how the world should work.

What we know to be "traditional" ways of banking and finance is under massive disruption. And only a few can see what's really happening.

I hope that with the sometimes-manic ramblings I've put to paper in this book, you have begun to gain an appreciation for what is really going on here.

I hope you understand the dramatic situation our governments, our central banks, our so-called democratically elected officials, deem is best for us, has ended up being worse for us.

I hope you understand that what you're told is the "way of the world" doesn't have to be. That the system that's rigged to the elites, the establishment, the "haves", the 1%, might work for them in its current form – but their own hubris will get in the way of them seeing what's happening under their noses.

The crypto revolution is a change that, in a century the world will look back on and marvel at those smart enough to have got on board early and put their full faith in a system that gives everyone a chance to do something great.

The decentralised nature of this revolution is shifting power financially and physically to the people. It's the ultimate libertarian, anti-establishment, anti-central authority change.

It's breaking the traditions we know and have relied on, and, that have failed us so badly.

It's a better way, a fairer way, and a way that could change the lives of people like you if you have the nous to do something about it. Take this as a motivational speech. Take it as an informative piece of work. Take it as a warning.

Things are changing, and it's happening now.

The crypto revolution is under way. It's just beginning. The opportunities are extraordinary. And it's changing the world in a way that we'll never see again, at least not in our lifetime. And perhaps not for another 100 years or more.

So you have just one choice to make.

Are you going to be a part of the crypto revolution, or not?

You decide.

Chapter 19: Libra: Facebook goes crypto

They went and did it., After much speculation and anticipation, **Facebook Inc. [NASDAQ:FB]** launched its own cryptocurrency and blockchain project. It calls the crypto "Libra" and it will exist on the Libra "blockchain".

Furthermore, it's also launching a user application and custody wallet it calls Calibra, that will be the portal between Libra and users.

What's clear is that Calibra will integrate with Facebook's WhatsApp and Messenger services, and also exist as a standalone app. Ultimately, down the track I see it also integrating seamlessly with Facebook itself along with Instagram.

There's plenty of hype and excitement amongst traditional financial "experts" about this move by Facebook. Some are calling it as the end of Bitcoin and crypto... Please, as if we haven't been here before with these "experts"!

Libra won't kill Bitcoin or crypto, if anything it's going to make them all exponentially better.

In many ways Libra will be a great thing, particularly in terms of bringing awareness of cryptocurrencies to billions of people. Think of it as a nice, easy step into the world of crypto for Facebook's billions of active users.

Furthermore, as Libra integrates itself with the wider crypto ecosystem and vice versa, I believe we'll see a large number of first-time crypto users through Libra finding their way into other cryptocurrencies, namely Bitcoin and some of the other major, useful and easy-to-use crypto.

Libra could be one of the biggest catalysts for the next crypto bull run we've seen – and I'll touch on that shortly.

But the thing is, for all the promise of Facebook's Libra, there are a few things you need to know that you're not getting the full story about. That's why I decided to dedicate a whole chapter to Facebook's move into crypto.

There are five key things you need to know about Facebook's Libra crypto that are integral to its impact on crypto markets long term and also the "traditional" banking and finance system.

And it's important that you understand how the big tech companies of the world are dying to go "full crypto".

1. It's a bigger immediate threat to banking than Bitcoin

Simple. Send money in seconds. Transfer money to friends and family at home or around the world, all using WhatsApp.

That's one of the main selling points from Facebook's crypto wallet application, Calibra. While much of the talk and hype is around Facebook's Libra cryptocurrency, the real core element here is the desire to open up "financial services" to the entire user base of Facebook's multi-faceted services.

That means delivering financial services whether it be payments and remittance, to other services I expect to see down the track from credit to investment products. The opening mission statement of Libra's white paper even says it's aiming to create, "a new opportunity for responsible financial services innovation".

The developers' paper on Libra goes on a little further to say they're looking to, "create a financial infrastructure that can foster innovation, lower barriers to entry, and improve access to financial services".

This isn't Facebook just getting on to the cryptocurrency mega-trend. This is Facebook getting into banking. The key difference and what you're not being told is that it's taking a run at banking the way the banks *should be doing it*. And for that, I actually give Facebook a little (very little) pat on the back.

Incumbent banks are very set in their ways. They have deep-seeded roots that span decades, and in some cases centuries.

That means they serve an important function in our current global financial system. Heck, they're part of the foundation of our "traditional" financial system. But it also means they are incredibly slow and resistant to change. In many cases they are more interested in maintaining the status quo rather than actually building a bank for the future.

That's where Facebook's move has such devastating reverberations for the incumbent banks. Facebook has the size and clout to step into global financial services, through Libra and Calibra, to deliver the kinds of financial services (new and old) that the incumbents can't.

In that sense Facebook is able to almost instantly reach out to its billions of active users and introduce them to a suite of financial products they've never had access to and likely never will from traditional banks.

As renowned and respected crypto guru Andreas M. Antonopoulos tweeted in June 2019:

> While Facebook's Libra doesn't compete against any open, public, permissionless, borderless, neutral, censorship-resistant blockchains, it *will* compete against both retail banks and central banks. This is going to be fun to watch.

Also, because of Facebook's size and reach it'll also be tapping into a future banking customer base that banks are desperate to corner for themselves.

Most people have very little understanding of how the global financial system works, very little idea of how a bank works. But they know how Facebook, WhatsApp, Messenger and Instagram work.

If you add payments, credit, financial products and services to billions of unbanked or underbanked individual, then you create possibly the world's largest financial institution.

Facebook is no longer the world's biggest social media company. Facebook is no longer the world's largest advertising company. Facebook is now becoming the world's largest and most powerful bank.

2. There's nothing decentralised about it

The whole point of a crypto network is decentralisation. A decentralised network is one that anyone on the network can contribute to the ongoing security and stability of that network. They do this by operating as a node on the network, an active participant. In effect a real decentralised network should allow for anyone to be a node, a validator on that network.

However, there are a number of features of Libra's "blockchain" that make it very clear not everyone can participate in that way. Furthermore, that control and stability is to be provided by a select few major corporations, of which Facebook intends to be one of these "Founding Members".

As Calibra's Customer Commitment paper explains:

> *Once the Libra network launches, Facebook, and its affiliates, will have the same commitments, privileges, and financial obligations as any other Founding Member. As one member among many, Facebook's role in governance of the association will be equal to that of its peers.*

Now when it speaks about "peers" it's really talking about massive global companies run by extremely wealthy, elite individuals. The kind of people that are desperate to get into crypto and now finally have a way to do it.

That's why Libra has implemented a strict set of rules to become a Founding Member and a validator on the Libra blockchain.

These Founding Member organisations are required to meet two of the following criteria:

Market value/customer balances:

- *Measure – More than $1 billion USD in market value or greater than $500 million USD customer balances.*

Scale

- *Measure – Reach greater than 20 million people a year, multinationally.*

Brand sustainability

- *Measure – Recognized as a top-100 industry leader by a third-party sector-specific association or media company. Examples of lists used to reference potential founding members include the Interbrand Global 100, the Fortune 500, the S&P Global 1200, the FTSE Eurotop 300, and other regional and country-specific lists that identify established brands.*

These Founding Members will be able to operate as validators on the Libra blockchain. In operating as a validator (node) they will play an active role in Libra's governance, they will receive rewards from the transactions on the network and they'll be eligible for dividends from the Libra Investment Token.

That's right, the Libra token is for the plebs – the Libra Investment Token is the juicy one that delivers ongoing returns and rewards, that's the one you want, and it's the one you can't have!

To get Libra Investment Tokens, these organisations need to buy their way in. And for doing so they get, "an expectation of returns from interest on the reserve, further incentivizing the validators to keep the system operational."

Libra has already said they need to make an investment of *at least* $10 million in the network through purchasing Libra Investment Tokens.

And some of the organisations that are already listed as Founding Members are MasterCard, PayPal, Visa, eBay,

Facebook (obviously), Lyft, Spotify, Uber, Vodafone, Coinbase, Xapo and Andreesen Horowitz.

They're all set to reap the rewards from the Libra Reserve, the Libra blockchain and the Libra tokens that the billions of Facebook users will end up buying.

You see, regular users will have to purchase Libra with fiat money. That money all goes into the Libra Reserve which will be in interest-bearing accounts, which flow back to the Libra Investment Token holders, not the actual users of Libra.

Let's make this nice and simple...

A giant multi-billion dollar organisation is creating a blockchain. It's invited and will get another bunch of giant multi-billion dollar organisations to participate in the network and decide on how it's run. These collections of giant multi-billion dollar organisations will all reap the benefits of the huge money generated by the everyday users of the network and the massive pool of investment funds backing it.

You get none of it.

Simple enough? Sound like a truly decentralised, fair, crypto network? Or does it just sound like a fancy way of shuffling around the current system that's almost set up exactly the same to benefit the already wealthy?

And let's also not forget that Facebook has been very coy about the economics of the Libra token. How many Libra tokens will ever exist? Will there even be a cap? Perhaps they'll just absorb fiat money until there's none left. What about if it starts adding non-cash investments? What happens if the value of the Libra Reserve crashes in a vicious bear market? Who's really controlling the kinds of investments and risk assets in the Libra Reserve?

These are all decisions and control that only Founding Members will have, which further emphasises that Libra isn't really for the end user, but a way to help giants of industry gather up more power and influence.

3. It's going to bring non-Libra cryptocurrency to the attention of billions of people

The exact numbers are a bit of a mystery, but most estimates have the number of unique, active Bitcoin wallets at around 30 million to 50 million. That means wallets in which there has been some kind of to and from transactions created.

Now that doesn't mean there's 30 million to 50 million individuals with wallets either. The likely number is much lower. For example, I have at least five Bitcoin wallet addresses that would be defined as active.

I'm not the average user, but even if the average Bitcoin user has at least two active Bitcoin wallets, then we're really only still talking about 15 million to 25 million individuals or organisations that have Bitcoin.

Do you have Bitcoin? Are you one of those 15 million to 25 million? You could go around and ask your friendship group or family who actually has any Bitcoin, and chances are it's not many of them.

And when you look at those numbers compared to the world's 7.5 billion population it works out that around 0.3% of the world actually hold any Bitcoin.

Now let's have a look at how many people use Facebook's WhatsApp and Messenger services (approx. at June 2019):

- WhatsApp – 1.6 billion active users.

- Facebook Messenger – 1.3 billion active users.

Again, it's fair to assume that most of those users actually use *both* WhatsApp and Messenger. So at worst there's still 1.6 billion active users of Facebook's two biggest owned messaging services.

I've pointed out these two in terms of numbers and not Facebook's 2.3 billion active users because it's WhatsApp and Messenger that Libra is going to integrate with first.

Either way, even if *just* 1.6 billion people are about to get direct exposure to cryptocurrency and a crypto wallet in the form of Calibra, that's a fair spike in global awareness of crypto.

1.6 billion people, or 21.3% of the world's population, are going to get a direct ramp from the traditional financial system into cryptocurrency. That's a 64-fold increase based on the number of active Bitcoin wallets.

Now you might think how that will impact other cryptocurrencies. Well it's simple. Once you have Libra tokens, I expect that it's only a matter of a very short time before there will be an exchange pair for Libra with crypto like BTC, ETH, XRP, LTC and many more.

That means the ease in which people can move from the traditional financial system into crypto like Bitcoin will become *exponentially easier*. And that's going to massively drive demand for crypto like Bitcoin, in my view.

Imagine if there's 64-times more demand for buying Bitcoin, and yet we know there's a finite supply of BTC. And considering BTC values are already starting to creep towards the US$10,000 mark again and potentially even closer to the 2017/18 highs of US$20,000 even before Libra launches... well this could be the catalyst that sends us into another gigantic crypto bull run.

And once you're down the crypto rabbit hole, it's hard to turn back. I'm saying that when you get a mass injection of interest and exposure to crypto, and you provide ways for people to then access something like Bitcoin, you open up a massive injection of demand in one hit that we might never see again.

4. The evil eye of the authorities still keeps watch

Immediately after Facebook announced it was going full crypto, lawmakers and authorities leapt out of the blocks with worries and concerns about Facebook's cryptocurrency. You see the sheer term "cryptocurrency" scares the living daylights out of most authorities and governments.

Immediately in France there was pushback. According to France24:

> [French] *Finance Minister Bruno Le Maire, whose government has also initiated a new tax on digital giants like Facebook that has angered the United States, said such digital money could never replace sovereign currencies.*
>
> *"It cannot and must not become a sovereign currency, with all of attributes of a currency" such as the capacity to issue sovereign debt and serve as a reserve currency.*
>
> *"The aspect of sovereignty must stay in the hands of states and not private companies which respond to private interests," Le Maire added.*
>
> *There need to be "guarantees" so that "this transaction instrument is not misused, for example, for the financing of terrorism or illicit activities," he said.*

That last bit is important. Government is constantly throwing out the national security card when it comes to innovation that threatens their power base, like cryptocurrency does. That's why they're going to enforce strict measures on Facebook to make sure they bend to the will of the authorities.

And we know that Facebook has already complied. As the material about Libra expressly explains when talking about how it manages user data:

> **Preventing fraud and criminal activity.**
>
> *Information may be shared to prevent malicious activity, such as instances of fraud, security threats, or criminal activity.*
>
> **Compliance with the law.**
>
> *Data may be shared to comply with legal or regulatory requirements, including sharing with law enforcement, regulators, and/or government*

officials, or in response to a valid legal request.

Payment processing and service providers.

When you authorize a payment, we share data with third parties necessary to process that transaction. We also share Calibra customer data with managed vendors and service providers – including Facebook, Inc.

If there is even suspicion of wrongdoing then all your user data could be shared with authorities, even if there's nothing going on. Furthermore, you will have to go through extensive "Know Your Client" (KYC) just to function with Libra and Calibra.

And, of course, Facebook hasn't got exactly a stellar record of how it treats customer data. And while Libra says it's separate and independent from Facebook, you have to question the motives when the "blockchain" is controlled by corporate entities.

After all, imagine all that data you have on social networks, and now imagine it all linked with your financial records, and now imagine it in one easy to locate place amongst a bunch of multi-billion dollar giants... Hang on, almost sounds like the existing financial system... and that's exactly why this isn't really a true cryptocurrency at heart.

Whereas with true crypto like Bitcoin you get that independence and freedom that you should have with your digital finances. For example, when you set up a Bitcoin wallet, you don't have to provide the controlling entities of Bitcoin with your personal information, because there are no controlling entities and there's no need for personal data attached to your wallet.

That's the soul of what cryptocurrency is about – it's so you can retain an element of control over your own data, privacy and finances. But the overseeing eye of Big Brother will want to ensure there's a way into Facebook's Libra and Calibra projects because it can't risk the fact these might end up with a lot of people using this as a pathway into other crypto, which it can't control.

Also we know that some jurisdictions like Australia are actively pressuring companies like Facebook to enable "backdoors" into encrypted messaging apps like WhatsApp again under the guise of "national security".

Australia's anti-encryption laws enable Australian authorities to compel companies to prove access to encrypted services, and they don't have to tell the users about it.

Now when you factor in the fact that Libra will be integrated within WhatsApp, it starts to get a little worrying about the power that government wields to track, trace and follow not just messaging data, but soon enough payment and wealth transfer data as well...

Or at least through Facebook's applications and systems.

The other thing that is no doubt hitting at the heart of global regulators is that Libra is going to be underpinned by financial "resources". Facebook goes some way to highlight Libra will be a database of programmable resources.

This leads me to think while its reserve will be "low-volatility assets, including bank deposits and government securities in currencies from stable and reputable central banks", it will also have scope for other assets it can tokenise to bolster the underlying asset backing Libra.

What it increasingly sounds like though is the International Monetary Fund's Special Drawing Rights (SDRs). Is Facebook trying to build out a "corporate SDR"? That's what it would look like on first appearances.

And there's a good chance that over time (a short time) Facebook's Libra does grow its user base and Libra Reserve to have significant sway as an alternative to the SDR. And if you don't think that is terrifying nation states, then you need to think again.

5. It is the most positive sign that Bitcoin and other

cryptocurrency is set to boom

For all the detail (and there's a lot of detail) around Libra and Calibra, there's still one core benefit that you simply can't ignore.

This is overall a good thing for the wider cryptocurrency ecosystem. Even if Libra does go on to be this quasi-hybrid financial instrument/cryptocurrency mutant and immensely popular, it's already brought the conversation of cryptocurrency to the masses.

In just one announcement Facebook has put cryptocurrency on the agenda of *billions of people*. Now for all the great things that the existing crypto community has been able to achieve since the birth of Bitcoin, that kind of reach it simply hasn't achieved yet.

And Facebook, in my view, is going to contribute to mass awareness, understanding and use of cryptocurrencies, not just Libra.

Think of Libra as the entry point, the portal through which the underbanked, the unbanked and even the banked-but-non-crypto-believers can now enter this amazing space.

Facebook might just be the catalyst that people now will begin to take cryptocurrency far more seriously than before. It takes a giant of industry to validate this as a legitimate opportunity to do something great for people to switch on to the opportunity.

It means that beyond Libra, beyond Bitcoin there will be crypto that will see a flow-on benefit from this wave of people that are soon to step into the crypto world for the first time.

And that means opportunity. Opportunity for these other cryptos to grow their own networks, their userbase, to expand and integrate their products, services, applications and technology into and with things like Libra.

I see the entire crypto ecosystem benefiting in greater flow of financial and human capital to innovate and continue the immense development in this space.

And if investors have got an early stake in the right crypto that are primed to ride this coming wave, I think they'll be set to mint crypto wealth, the likes of which we've never seen before. But time is running out, with around 1.6 billion people about to flood the crypto space you don't want to be at the back of that queue!

That's why it's so important to understand the benefits that Facebook's crypto play brings, as well as the real facts about how it's set up and will operate. While it's no "Bitcoin killer" in my view, it certainly has the potential to bridge the gap between crypto as we know it today and billions of new crypto users that I think are set to flood the crypto markets, all thanks to our controversial friends at Facebook.

Chapter 20: The regret of a lifetime

To perhaps nudge you that final step further into the crypto world, let me leave you with one final story. A personal story and one that holds great regrets. But as much as it hurts to recount this story over and over again, it serves as a lesson.

The lesson is to have faith and conviction in your views and beliefs. When your gut tells you one thing and your brain tells you another, perhaps you should listen to your gut.

I didn't in this story, and I should have. And I will never make the same mistakes again.

***

I sat outside the Nasi Padang Indonesian restaurant on Swanston Street, Melbourne, Australia. It was around May 2011.

I'd always had a deep enthusiasm for all things technology related. Computers, audio players, video games, robotics, cars, mechanics, electronics, everything that had a beating heart of a machine was fascinating to me.

Sometimes I even had to double-check to make sure I wasn't some kind of advance AI, a cyborg. For your information, I'm not. But could I be...

That day was surprisingly warm. Melbourne around May is usually cold. But at any time of the year it can be a four-seasons-in-a-day kind of place. It can be cold and windy early in the morning. But lunchtime the sun breaks through and you could be sitting outside in the sunshine on a nice 20 degree Celsius day – in autumn! Then by the run home it's pelting down with rain, maybe some hail, and it seems like Mother Nature has just decided it's time to end everything.

Fortunately, this lunchtime it was sunny enough to sit outside. Must have been around 20 degrees, because I remember I was sat down on the pavement, suit jacket off. While I'd probably do that even if it were 10 degrees Celsius, I wouldn't have done so outside.

I had ordered the prawn pad thai. It's the only thing I ever ordered from there. It was good, the best in the area. It was also my local because I owned an apartment in the building it was in. I was several levels up, and a short lift ride and walk through the foyer had me on the doorstep.

This lunchtime, however, I hadn't decided to go home for lunch. Sandwiches would have to wait. Instead I was waiting for my work colleague Daryn. At the time I was toiling away as a financial adviser for a Melbourne-based financial services company. A great company full of brilliant people. A young company, so many of the staff were friends and hung out in social circles outside the office.

Daryn was the kind of guy where we both seemed to share similar views on life, the world, the economy, finance. He also had the same inclination to technology. We got chatting about the usual things, finance, some clients, the global financial system. Remember, we were just a year off the back of the global financial crisis, so it was still topical. We both still had clients reeling from massive losses thanks to the devastation across global markets and at home on the Australian Stock Exchange.

We were always looking for opportunity. We both knew that great opportunity came in times after catastrophic failure. And there had been no greater catastrophic failure than that of the global debt markets and the global financial system.

Through my own personal research and mulling around online I had come across this strange digital currency called "Bitcoin". My first experiences with it had been a while ago. Actually back in 2010.

It had popped up a couple of times on various forums, and people kept directing others into the "deep web" to find out more about it and how to get it.

The key concepts were that it was anonymous and that you could get it by "mining it". And, most importantly, you could use it to buy things. I had read about a guy in a

Bitcoin forum from Jacksonville, Florida, who had offered up 10,000 Bitcoins to buy a couple of pizzas. The guy who went by the forum handle "Laszlo" offered up the bounty to anyone who would get him a couple of pizzas and deliver them to him.

At the time another forum user pointed out they were expensive pizzas because the Bitcoin USD exchange rate meant 10,000 BTC was around US$41. A few days after his offer, Laszlo was happy to report he was successful in his trade of 10,000 BTC for his pizza.

But through most of 2010 it was just an interesting idea. More or less worthless, and seemingly the instrument of those that knew far more about computer programming and coding than I did.

So for the rest of 2010 it just remained there, in the back of my mind floating around, occasionally popping up again in some research. Then things started to progress and it started to be available for trade, exchange, more readily available for use, and more people were starting to get involved in the mining of it.

It really was a way to print your own money. And with the US government going through their initial stages of quantitative easing I was starting to ask the question, if it could print money, why can't I? With Bitcoin, in those early days, we actually could print our own money.

So I invited Daryn to lunch to chat about Bitcoin and perhaps look at a way we could both get involved and start mining some, and maybe have it be worth something that we could exchange back to Aussie money.

I told Daryn that I wanted to chat about an opportunity that was risky, complicated and new, but ultimately it was a licence to print money. And we talked.

(The following is a paraphrase of the conversation we actually had. But this was our first instance of talking about how Bitcoin works and ways in which we could get involved...)

"Daryn, I want to chat to you about this currency thing, Bitcoin. I think there could be an opportunity here.

From what I understand you can print your own money. Seriously. Using a computer you can 'mine' these coins that are actually worth real money. Currently you can exchange them for USD. Now here's the thing, each one is worth about US$1 right now and every time you 'mine' a block of coins, you get 50 coins. That's US$50 for doing nothing except running a computer program. Around a year ago you could mine them and they were worth about 7 cents per Bitcoin – so around $3.50 for each block."

Daryn asked again about the mining side of things. He wasn't quite sure about how you could just mine these blocks from thin air using a computer, and just create money from what was effectively nothing.

I repeated the process and again explained by mining a block using a computer you would get 50 coins as a reward. And at current prices it would be worth $150.

There was a strange silence between us as we both took the time to absorb the opportunity. We could clearly see that this was a real thing. But we also both had extensive education in finance and economics. We were both employed in the financial advice industry and were both extremely familiar with traditional and non-traditional markets and financial instruments.

Importantly, we'd both just witnessed first-hand what happens when complex financial instruments go wrong – people lose money. A lot of money.

Now here in front of us (well, at the forefront of our discussion) was something completely new, very foreign to Daryn, very interesting to us both and seemingly too good to be true. We both knew there was no such thing as a "money tree". Everyone knows this to be true. And in terms of printing your own money, well unless you were a central bank, that wasn't going to happen.

But this was exactly the potential of Bitcoin. Every ounce of our financial experience and knowledge said that this wasn't real, it couldn't be. But it was. To us Bitcoin was hen's teeth, the golden egg, a unicorn, the pot at the end of the rainbow. This new thing, Bitcoin, was in fact a money tree.

We finished up lunch as we both had clients to get back to. We made note that we'd chat about it more. Sit on it for a bit, research a bit more and find out in far more detail how this would work from an economic point of view.

About a week later we chatted more about it. We threw around how we would go about things. We to'd and fro'd about it. And we kept this ongoing discussion going for a couple more weeks; all the while keeping an eye on the price of Bitcoin.

Before we knew it Bitcoin was worth more than US$20. Then in early June the price punched through US$30. We had seen the price go nuts, in the space of just a month it was up another 1,000%.

The longer we waited the more expensive one Bitcoin became. When we first started talking a few months earlier just one block would have seen us earn US$150. By now that same block would be worth US$1,500. If we were faster, earlier, it's likely we would already have covered our initial costs.

We had another chat about things, very serious about what to do now. By this stage Daryn had done some more research, and I had gone to some length understanding how to set up a computer to mine Bitcoin. I tried to get my head around how to get a "client" and to set it up on a computer using an array of GPUs to mine Bitcoin effectively enough so as to be competitive enough to actually get some blocks.

At this point we had figured out that to mine Bitcoin was going to require two key things:

1. A powerful computer.

2. Energy.

You see, by this point we clearly weren't the only people looking at and mining Bitcoin. Experienced campaigners were already mining it with computer rigs they had already set up with multiple GPUs.

The use of GPUs was critical. They were able to mine faster and harder than any normal computer CPU. That meant building a custom PC. And to be competitive with other miners we needed some serious hardware. That meant also buying the equipment that was going to set us back around $1,500-$2,000 at the time.

We figured that way we would have enough GPU power to be competitive enough to mine and be successful in achieving Bitcoin blocks. But then we analysed the situation further.

We would have to run the computer 24/7 to be really efficient. And a tricked up custom computer wasn't cheap to run. Somehow we would have to wear the energy bills too. But with the price of Bitcoin it was looking like that wouldn't matter. At this rate, after a few weeks we should be able to get a block or two and meet our costs for the whole year.

That was it. We would source the parts needed and build a custom computer. I had a spare room in my apartment. We'd set it up in there and have the beast running 24/7. By the end of the year we'd probably have built up a few thousand in returns. Worst-case scenario, we'd have blown $2,000 and own a pretty great gaming computer.

We went away to price up and get the parts needed to build our Bitcoin mining "rig". And then the price of Bitcoin started to fall. And then it fell a little further, and then further still. We put the plans on hold to see how this was going to pan out.

By mid-October Bitcoin had plummeted from over US$30 to around US$2.20. It floated around this US$2 to US$3 range for the rest of the year. It was at this point we decided to flick the idea of building a custom rig to run 24/7.

Doing the sums on the current price, and the outlay, it didn't make sense. We both figured we'd be better off investing that money into stocks instead and generating a return from the good old traditional ASX.

However, we weren't completely dead on the idea just yet. We also toyed with the idea of just buying some Bitcoin outright.

Sure, we wouldn't become miners. That didn't make economic sense. But nothing would stop us from just going to a Bitcoin exchange and buying $1,500 worth and sitting them somewhere to see what happens.

Once more our education and experience got the better of us. I had seen Bitcoin go from 7 US cents to US$1 to US$30 and all the way back to US$2 in the space of a bit over a year. That kind of volatility suits *no one.* Let alone two finance professionals with common sense and a background in investing.

Again we thought about the opportunity cost of $1,500 worth of Bitcoin today versus $1,500 of stock investment instead. With Bitcoin worth a couple of bucks and the potential to continue to crash back down to nothing but cents, we took the "smarter" approach and stuck with what we knew.

Add to the fact that, while in theory at this time buying Bitcoin and storing it outright seemed easy, it wasn't. This was early doors for the breakthrough technology. The exchanges were dodgy at best, the people you were buying from you never knew, there were no faces, no risk-free transactions. We could very well exchange $1,500 and get nothing. The risk was simply far too high at the time, based on the potential return that we believed was possible.

We were quite comfortable with our decision through almost all of 2012. Bitcoin fell off the radar from the mainstream. The price "stabilised" and was worth around US$5, $6 for most of the year. Sure it still doubled from US$3, but so did plenty of ASX-listed companies too.

Bitcoin, while a great idea, a great technology and possibly something that would stick around for a long time, was just a thing. It didn't really have financial merit for investment. It didn't really make sense on the numbers to mine it. And the number of people mining had exponentially increased by then, anyway. There were now mining "pools" where users pooled resources to mine Bitcoins. Some people were putting YouTube videos online showing entire *rooms of GPUs* strung together into one super-mining-rig.

There was no way we would be able to compete with that. And the more miners there were, the more power they had, the less chance we had of even mining a single block.

By late 2012 the number of Bitcoins you would get as reward for mining a block halved, as explained earlier in this book, in the chapter "Events that changed Bitcoin forever".

This all pointed to a situation that simply didn't make sense in the "traditional financial rules and principles sense" for Daryn or I to really start mining or buy up Bitcoins.

We had the opportunity. We were there at the right time. But we didn't see it for what it truly was. We focused too much on the now and not enough on the future. We got caught up in its wild price swings and didn't understand the real potential.

Had we started mining in 2011 or even just spent $2,000 on some Bitcoins at US$2.20 today, we'd be sitting on a Bitcoin fortune of around US$1.01 million.

I need a moment...

Every time I tell this story it's hard. And I always need a moment. And I'll likely kick myself until the day I die about the opportunity to change our lives that went begging. I will never have such short-nose vision on a life-changing opportunity ever again.

The truth is, I might never see an opportunity like that again.

So be it.

But in 2011 we didn't anticipate the world was almost coming to another global financial crisis. And we certainly didn't think that just two years later, one block of 50 Bitcoins that we could have mined would be worth US$57,362.50. We didn't foresee that action could have resulted in us sitting on millions' worth of digital gold.

Simply, we were wrong. I was wrong. And in 2013 when Bitcoin breached through US$1,100 I vowed to never underestimate an opportunity of that magnitude ever again.

And therein lies the purpose to this story. Learn from the mistakes of others. I don't tell you about my great "could have" moment for fun. It pains me every time I recount it.

I tell you this story to show you that great opportunity exists with the right knowledge and the right information. But perhaps more important is the right action to take when you have the conviction to back yourself and take a little risk for potentially life-changing reward.

Don't do what we did and convince yourself out of an opportunity because "traditional" thinking says so. Be outside the box; think outside the box and act outside the box.

Those that do, those that did, went on to make millions from Bitcoin. Many have become Bitcoin entrepreneurs. Some, like me, missed it, didn't properly see it.

It helped define my view on opportunity, and my ability to back my conviction when I see opportunity. And that's why I wrote this book. To educate you to the opportunity that *exists* with Bitcoin and cryptocurrency.

And in every part of my research into Bitcoin, every part of the time spent investigating, experimenting and uncovering the traps and trimmings of the cryptocurrency world, it all points to a hugely exciting future. Every part of me says that this *is the future*. And that if you take anything from my final story it's to not make the same mistakes.

If you believe in this revolution as much as I do, then by all means do what you can to get involved.

And instead of having regrets, you'll be thanking me one day for pointing you in the right direction. The direction to change your life, by getting involved, investing, using, buying, selling, and immersing yourself in the world of Bitcoin, cryptocurrency and the cryptoconomy.

About the publishers...

Southbank Investment Research

Thank you for reading.

I want to tell you a little bit about our business and why we published Sam's book.

Southbank Investment Research is like a private intelligence network with a simple but profound mission...

To find alternative ways to grow your money.

To pinpoint opportunities you won't hear about from mainstream sources.

Share ideas that could change your life for the better.

We're proud to share alternative ideas because we know that these are the kinds of ideas that change people's lives.

Crypto Revolution perfectly fits into that mission.

It marks the culmination of what we are trying to achieve for our readers:

Confident control of your own wealth. Another weapon in your arsenal to give you an advantage over other investors.

So we think everyone should know about it. That is why we have made the book available at such a low cost. We believe our work is valuable – so the best thing for us is to let you see it for yourself with as little fuss as possible – then decide for yourself.

And it couldn't be better timed: 2019 looks to be the perfect moment to get clued up on cryptocurrencies.

If you would like to take that journey further and get regular insight and crypto opportunities sent directly to your inbox, visit www.Crypto-Rev.co.uk.

As a company, we stick by a set of core principles:

INDEPENDENCE ALWAYS BEATS DEPENDENCE

Anyone who finds our work already knows this in their gut. We're not money managers. We're publishers. We're not taking your money and managing it (dependence), we're giving you the tools you need to independently manage it for yourself.

This matters. It matters a hell of a lot. And not just because by taking charge of your own finances – or as much of them as you can – will likely lead to better investment outcome.

Taking control and responsibility of your own life doesn't imply you don't care about other people. Wanting to solve your own problems doesn't mean you don't care about other people. But cherishing independence instead of seeking dependence leads to better investments and better outcomes.

GROUPTHINK IS DEATH

The trend towards censorship and suppression of free speech is terrifying. It doesn't matter if it's Google de-platforming people, mainstream media branding ideas that don't fit a narrow worldview as "populism", or university students seeking to silence speakers they don't agree with. At its roots it's all groupthink. It all risks letting other people tell you what you can and can't think. And you have to fight it.

There are very practical investment implications of that idea too.

Groupthink is the reason most people are incapable of

buying at the bottom and selling at the top. In fact they do the opposite. They ignore assets when they're cheap, hated and ignored and buy them when they're at the top, when everyone else is buying. That's groupthink in action again. It's emotional, group-led investing, instead of rational, individual action.

It's why Southbank Investment Research will never have a "house view" – the risk of that becoming infected by groupthink is just too high. Better to have a range of competing viewpoints – at the very least, it keeps everyone honest and thinking critically. At best, it protects you (the reader) from slipping into groupthink.

SEEK THE TRUTH

Efficient market theorists tell you that the reason most investors don't beat the market is because markets are always perfectly priced. In this model, anyone that *does* beat the market is just lucky.

The same goes when people analyse politics, technology and other world events. Very few people saw the global financial crisis coming. Therefore anyone who did must have been *lucky.* It was random!

The same goes for "black swan" events like the election of Donald Trump. Most people didn't forecast it. Only a few people took it seriously enough to see what was happening. Luck, again.

In truth? This simply isn't the case.

If some people beat the market consistently, it's worth understanding how that's possible, rather than deciding it was random. The same goes for major world events like the financial crisis. How come some people saw it coming when most didn't?

It comes down to a willingness to think critically – and to seek the truth. There were people out there in 2005 and

2006 who were highlighting the fact that the US housing market was creating dangerous fragility (Dan Denning, founder of Southbank Investment Research was one of them).

The problem wasn't that no one saw it coming. It was the fact that the people who *did* were ignored, marginalised or branded "scaremongers" by the mainstream. You have to be willing to seek the truth – seek ideas on the fringe people have discounted. You may run the risk of looking stupid in the short term.

But in the long term... truth seekers win.

That's why we work with the very best of the best financial thinkers, writers and analysts.

And that's the *exact* underlying mechanics of our decision to publish *Crypto Revolution*.

In our view, Sam Volkering is the top man in this exciting new field. Taking his lead could be hugely beneficial to you down the line.

If you would like to know more about Southbank Investment Research, visit us at:
www.southbankresearch.com.

Good investing,

Nick O'Connor
Publisher, Southbank Investment Research

Want to take your crypto investing further?

And get ongoing ideas, analysis, podcasts... and the <u>names</u> of the NEXT coins that could return you 20, 50, even 100 times your money?

All sent directly to your inbox?

Go to Crypto-Rev.co.uk or scan the QR code below and take advantage of a limited opportunity to profit from the crypto eruption.